AWAKENING TO NATURE

RENEWING YOUR LIFE

BY CONNECTING

WITH THE NATURAL WORLD

CHARLES COOK

CONTEMPORARY BOOKS

Library of Congress Cataloging-in-Publication Data

Cook, Charles, 1945–
    Awakening to nature : renewing your life by connecting with the natural
world / Charles Cook.
       p.   cm.
    ISBN 0-8092-2399-6
    1. Nature.   2. Human ecology.   3. Natural history.   I. Title.

QH81.C745   2001
508—dc21   00-64349

Contemporary Books

A Division of The **McGraw-Hill** Companies

1 2 3 4 5 6 7 8 9 0   AGM/AGM   0 9 8 7 6 5 4 3 2 1

ISBN 0-8092-2399-6

This book was set in Adobe Jenson
Printed and bound by Quebecor-Martinsburg

Cover design by Monica Baziuk
Cover photo copyright © Ed Dimsdale/Photonica

McGraw-Hill books are available at special quantity discounts to use as premiums
and sales promotions, or for use in corporate training programs. For more
information, please write to the Director of Special Sales, Professional Publishing,
McGraw-Hill, Two Penn Plaza, New York, NY 10121-2298. Or contact your local
bookstore.

This book is printed on acid-free paper.

This book is dedicated to everyone who longs to reconnect
with the wild heart and soul of nature

CONTENTS

❦ PART II ❧

COMMUNING WITH NATURE

INTRODUCTION

YOUR DEEPEST ROOTS are in nature. No matter who you are, where you live, or what kind of life you lead, you remain irrevocably linked with the rest of creation. Your ancestors arose and evolved within the heart of the natural world; nature is the birthplace and spiritual home of your species. Whether you're aware of it or not, you still have a vital need for regular, meaningful contact with this nourishing realm.

Your predecessors shared the natural landscape with an extremely rich and diverse community of life, and within this vibrant universe the defining characteristics, unique qualities, and current potentialities of human beings were molded. Hundreds of millennia of nature-based living helped shape your genetic and physical makeup, your instincts and intuitions, your emotions and desires, and your spiritual longings.

Consider the increasingly synthetic and frenetic world we occupy now, which couldn't be more different from that of our origins. It's not surprising that some of us feel like displaced persons, partly because our society changes more rapidly than we can easily adapt to, and it leaves some of our essential nonmaterial needs unmet. Of course, our consumer culture provides us with countless pleasures and benefits, which is why most of us remain loyal subjects; but it also gives short shrift to nature and promotes technology-mediated living. Nature-based ways have been abandoned, and most of us spend the bulk of our waking hours indoors, occupying artificial spaces and surrounded by countless products of the human mind. Not coincidently, our lives have become more stressful, unbalanced, and unhealthy.

Such changes are extremely recent for the human species, so they've barely begun to alter our basic makeup. If we were somehow to come face-to-face with our early ancestors, we initially would have trouble communicating with them, and the cultural and technological gaps between us would be enormous, but we would probably discover that most of our fundamental needs remain similar.

Nature still runs rampant in our bloodstreams and souls, no matter how many layers of civilization we impose on ourselves, how many years of education we undergo, how many technologies we surround ourselves with, or how many walls we build to isolate, insulate, and protect ourselves from the wild. Some of us know and feel this instinctively, but there are also forces in our world that encourage us to dissociate ourselves from the deeper realities of who we are and what we need in life.

Although separating ourselves from nature won't necessarily prove fatal, at least in the short run, we can expect to eventually pay a steep price psychologically, emotionally, and spiritually. The overall quality and depth of our lives are certain to be diminished when we're cut off from nature, and we're less likely to feel at home here on earth, although we might not always recognize what's missing. Becoming a reasonably whole and contented human being is never easy nor guaranteed in this life, where the obstacles of the modern world are many and daunting, but it's especially difficult when we lack regular access to the beauty, inspiration, meaning, and sustenance of the natural realm.

Perhaps you don't need convincing. Most of us harbor positive associations and feelings about nature, and some of us are fortunate to have had experiences that helped us bond with the natural world. Few of us are immune to nature's attractions, although not everyone may acknowledge it; recognizing one's need or love for nature in a culture that devalues it can be painful. If we're willing to venture out, though, how many of us can resist the sensory delights of wild nature, especially when the natural landscape is in full bloom, or fail to feel excitement when encountering wildlife? Who among us hasn't sometimes longed to flee our stuffy spaces for the wilder, greener, more peaceful places of nature, or fantasized about abandoning the rat race and relocating to a tropical island or a mountaintop retreat?

Indeed, you'd have to be seriously numbed or alienated to be incapable of responding to the natural world. Imagine being left cold by a spectacular mountain or canyon vista, or the piercing music of birdsong, or the pounding of ocean surf on a windy day, or sweet meadow fragrances, or the warmth of the sun's rays in early spring, or the impossibly rich colors of fall foliage, or the mesmerizing roar of a waterfall, or the weird harmonies of a chorus of coyotes, or the wide-eyed stare of an elk at close range, or the sight of waterfowl gracefully taking flight from a wild lake, or an open view of the vast glittering night sky . . .

So much of what makes up the natural world resonates with us, stirs us, or soothes us. A few elements may irritate or frighten us, especially at first, but most negative reactions fade with experience. Deep in our bones we still possess a strong, species-wide affinity for other living things, and many of us find we're most content when we have close, frequent contact or communion with the natural world. Nature is like food for us—nourishment for the body, the senses, the mind, the spirit, the soul.

What then is to be done about our predicament as citizens of a de-natured culture? The challenge we face is clear: how can we ever live successfully and sanely in this society, which requires so much time and energy for most of us to meet our basic needs, and still maintain a meaningful relationship with nature? The solutions may not be entirely simple or easy to carry out, but most of us can unquestionably do much more to integrate nature into our lives. One of the purposes of this book is to show you how.

No, you don't need to drop out, relocate permanently to a remote wilderness area, and take up residence in a tent in order to develop a deeper relationship with the natural world. Nor do you have to make great sacrifices or invest huge amounts of time, although the more hours you can spend in natural surroundings, the more you're probably going to benefit. You may want to change some elements of your life to make it more nature-friendly, but the choices are entirely yours to make. If you're a city dweller, you should find a number of options available close to home. Wherever you happen to live, be aware that connecting with nature can be so gratifying that it might become one of the most important and meaningful relationships you know.

And can you really afford to do otherwise? Modern life with its manic pace obviously has the makings of an extremely stressful journey. Fortunately, nature provides a perfect antidote to many of the imbalances, absurdities, and insanities—offering limitless opportunities for relaxation, solitude, contact with countless other living things, the exploration of lovely scenery, and as much exercise as we want. Our health, well-being, and state of mind can only benefit—as can our spiritual life, our sense of meaning, and our ability to know life as something much richer and deeper than the often limiting experiences of everyday existence.

Because of the radically new ways human beings have learned to live in modern times, which have led to such a diminished relationship with the natural world, our culture has come to think and speak of nature as something totally separate from us. Such a concept is alien, of course, to the indigenous peoples of the world. It's actually an error in perception to see nature as "other." Your body is as nature-based as that of any animal in the wild. Every particle in every cell of your body comes from nature. Every aspect of your physical and emotional makeup has evolved over time in the course of your ancestors' interactions with the elements of the primordial landscape. That we consider nature to be a completely separate entity is one of many signs of our disconnection from the earth.

As a culture, we also shrink from acknowledging that we're dependent in any way upon nature or the workings of the living world. This is another indication of our alienation, and it helps explain how we've been able to engage in such self-destructive practices as poisoning our own water and air and exploiting other precious natural resources. However, it's obvious that we're fully a part of the earth's web of life and can't possibly exist without it, regardless of how civilized we supposedly are or how self-sufficient and independent we may feel.

None of us can breathe without the oxygen exhaled by trillions of trees and other plants that blanket the surface of this beautiful blue-green planet. Nor can we live without a stream of clean water flowing through our bodies. Nor will we exist for long without the intake of food furnished by the earth's flora and fauna. Our long-term survival and that of other species depend on our adoption of a more planet-respecting perspective—one that acknowledges our dependence upon the earth's ecosystems and embraces the knowledge and wisdom that our well-being is invariably interconnected with that of other living things.

Stop for a moment and take a look out the nearest window. Notice what predominates in the view before your eyes. Is it nature or the man-made world that prevails? Or a mix of both? If the vista is mainly natural and it's available to you on a daily basis, you have something to be thankful for; merely having regular visual access to nature can benefit your life in a number of ways. Now try an easy exercise, if you're so inclined and assuming a few elements of nature are within sight: spend a few minutes simply gazing out, resting your eyes on whatever natural forms you see. Then notice your thoughts and feelings. Has your mind become quieter? Is your body more relaxed? Is there any detectable improvement in your mood?

As you may already know, it's difficult to stay stressed out or maintain a negative mood while quietly focusing or meditating on nature. You'll often feel noticeably better after spending even a short time soaking in some natural scenery. The positive effects will be magnified when you actually get outdoors and interact directly with nature. For example, simply walking in the woods or sitting in the grass (the quieter and more secluded the area, the better) is capable of markedly improving your state of mind and, if you're sufficiently receptive, sometimes transforming it.

The truth is there's no healthier or more effective way to temporarily disconnect from everyday stress—and at the same time raise your spirits—than by removing yourself from the confinement of the four-walled world and immersing yourself in nature. Even a fifteen-minute break or an hour at lunchtime can help; a much longer period is preferable whenever possible, especially if you're someone who's suffering from nature-deprivation, overwork, or burnout. Large natural areas are ideal, but even the smallest city park will sometimes offer a gratifying degree of respite and restoration.

Recreating or resting in nature won't solve all your problems, of course, and the difficulties of the day will usually await your return. You'll sometimes find, though, that troubles shrink to more manageable sizes while you're away, and you can later view them "through fresh eyes" from a more balanced perspective affected by your experiences in nature.

At the same time, you don't need to be a nervous wreck to reap rewards from spending time in the natural world. Feeling at one with the universe, or uncommonly happy should you be so fortunate, certainly doesn't require you to stay home; nature is one of the best places to be when you're in such a mood. Whatever your circumstances or state of mind, you'll find no ceiling on the potential benefits you can tap into in nature.

The positive effects of spending time in the wild are many; some are subtle, others more striking. For example, regular contact with nature is capable of enriching the content and quality of our dreams, stimulating an intensified sense of aliveness, eliciting feelings of excitement and joy, and awakening in us a strong awareness of our close relatedness to other living beings—resulting in a much deeper connection with our wilder "brethren." We may be inspired to engage in soulful inner explorations that can lead to major improvements in our lives.

Some of us find ourselves falling into a passionate, lifelong love affair with nature. Others develop a more sober respect, seeking out nature for wisdom as one would a great teacher or mentor. Still others are filled with a feeling of profound reverence in nature's presence and come to see her extraordinary manifestations as expressions of god or spirit.

Our inner experiences in nature aren't always easily conveyed to the uninitiated. Skeptics abound in our culture, of course, and some will assume our epiphanies are merely the effects of being exposed to such pleasurable and healthful elements as fresh air, sunshine, exercise, lovely scenery, and being able to rub elbows with an array of interesting living things. It's hard for those who have no firsthand experience to understand that such an underadvertised and underappreciated realm as the natural world can actually offer some of the deepest satisfactions, fulfillments, and sources of meaning available to us.

To those who are used to finding life a constant struggle or have been taught that everything comes at a price, some of the rewards may sound too easy to achieve and too good to be true. After all, these benefits are totally free and available to anyone who knows how to reap them. Our culture's complicated requirements don't apply. We're often taught, especially by our media, to view the wild as a dangerous place, and at first we may have difficulty accepting the truth that nature is actually safer in many respects than civilization. Of course, we need to know how to take care of ourselves there; nature can be unforgiving to those who are reckless or unprepared. However, with the proper know-how, the risks are minimal and the rewards infinite.

The kinds of benefits that come more easily than we expect include feeling unaccountably high or ecstatic "without having done anything" except sit quietly in a pristine setting, or experiencing a deep sense of connectedness with other life-forms, or discovering easy yet profound insights into complex problems, or finding our consciousness flooded with an overwhelming feeling of peacefulness. Science might be able to offer some possible explanations, but many mysteries remain in nature and life. Thankfully, we don't need to fully understand what happens to us in the wild to be deeply affected or changed by it.

So how do we get started? Where do those of us who have been living a relatively nature-deficient life begin? How is it possible to get on a more nature-oriented path? How might we invite nature into our daily lives? What can we do to develop a meaningful and lasting personal relationship with nature?

Probably the most basic and obvious action some of us need to take is to make more room for nature in our everyday lives—to allot more time in our schedule to be outdoors. If you don't already spend at least a few hours in the natural world each week, try to start doing so now. A minimum of an hour or more each day would be ideal, along with some weekends devoted to nature-based recreation or leisure.

But if visiting nature on a regular basis is currently impossible for you, or if transporting yourself to a natural area is problematic, don't despair. In a later chapter will be a discussion on how to maintain a connection with nature when you're stuck indoors and unable to get out often. If an overload of work is keeping you inside, incidently, how about transporting some tasks, such as paperwork or reading, to a nearby park? You're sure to benefit from being there no matter what you're doing.

The options open to us in the wilder places are almost unlimited. A few of the possibilities include such ordinary everyday activities as walking, picnicking, and socializing with family or friends; participating in more adventurous and physically demanding pursuits like hiking, canoeing, rafting, cycling, or horseback riding, either for the day or while camping out; engaging in bird-watching, identifying plants, animal tracking, and other nature studies; and experiencing the natural world in more contemplative ways such as meditating or quietly communing with nature. Many of the choices that are available to us will be examined in this book.

While almost anything we do in a natural setting can help us feel more connected, there are ways we can intentionally increase and intensify our awareness. These will be invaluable in helping us fully awaken to nature, which offers the potential of renewing or transforming our lives. Throughout this book are many ideas and suggestions that will assist you in getting closer to and communing with the natural world, including a number of explorations of various elements of nature in Part II.

Have you ever spent time consciously communing with nature? If not, it's time to try. Have you ever been immersed in the natural world for an entire day or longer, completely free of everyday distractions? This, too, should be on your agenda. Do you know what it's like to relax in a natural setting without needing to accomplish anything? It's a way to unwind more completely than some of us have ever experienced. Not to criticize goal-oriented behavior, but some of us have been so indoctrinated in the importance of productivity, believing we must always have "something to show for our day," that we're incapable of taking time off for ourselves to totally relax.

Have you ever had the experience of feeling "at one with nature"? Have you ever felt like a full-fledged member of the natural order and not merely a lone individual in search of personal contentment? With a surprisingly small amount of effort on your part, these experiences await you. Imagine what it might be like to feel intensely alive and aware, with your senses wide open, yet calmly and completely in harmony with your surroundings. Imagine being unhurried and undistracted, with a deep sense of relatedness to the natural world, as if you were fully a part of the living, breathing landscape yet still a citizen of the human community. If you find this hard to visualize, fear not. We're all capable of expanding our horizons and boundaries to encompass nature.

Try to also imagine what it might be like to absorb some of nature's vital energies into your body, mind, and spirit on a regular basis and bring them back home with you. Imagine becoming more completely grounded and connected with the earth. Can you sense how your inner life might be enriched by your experiences in nature? How they might enliven your participation in the human drama? How your whole being might be strengthened or healed? How you might be inspired to live more fully and deeply?

Whatever steps you need to take to make room for nature in your life won't feel like a sacrifice, at least not for long. The rewards you'll receive from connecting with the natural world are more reliable than most things in life, and they'll be quickly self-reinforcing. Anything you give up is almost guaranteed to be greatly outweighed by the gifts you'll gain.

What happens to us out there in the wild sometimes seems magical, but it's also wise to refrain from idealizing or sentimentalizing nature. Life perpetually preys on other life, after all, and harshness as well as suffering is a part of the total picture. Yet it's impossible to overestimate what the natural world has to offer us. Among other considerations, many of the missing pieces and answers to personal and societal problems tend to turn up there. Nature is a place where a more complete perspective on life can be acquired, where invaluable wisdom awaits the sincere seeker. Ultimately, beyond the splendid landscapes, the fascinating forms, the interesting flora and fauna, and other external enticements lies one of the most meaningful, spiritually expansive, and sacred places we'll ever know—where human beings still belong, although too many of us have lost touch with this truth. Enter this land and your life can only be enriched.

How to Use This Book

THE PURPOSE OF THIS BOOK is to help you connect with nature. In the chapters that follow you'll find hundreds of ideas, thoughts, and suggestions intended to assist and inspire you— whether you're a total beginner or a seasoned devotee—to cultivate a more meaningful relationship with the natural world, integrate nature more completely into your life, and experience more fully the joys and benefits of communing with the wild.

Although the chapters may be read sequentially, which is indeed advisable in Part I for those who are inexperienced in the natural world, this isn't essential. Some nature-related topics may be of more interest to you than others, so feel free to skip around as much as you like. Pay special attention to any subject matter that resonates strongly for you. While the book may be read for pleasure, you're encouraged to use it in a way that energizes and motivates you to interact with nature.

The twelve chapters of Part I, "Getting Closer to Nature," address a broad range of subjects related to the process of connecting with nature, focusing particularly on how you can come more into community with the natural world. Chapter 1 briefly considers our roots in nature, looking critically at how astray our culture and civilization may have gone. Chapters 2 through 12 address such topics as how to find more room in our lives for nature, preparatory steps we can all take, how to invite nature into our indoor spaces, the importance of getting outside, nature-related options close to home, how to ground ourselves on the earth, outdoor recreation, more meditative ways of being in nature, wilderness activities, the world of our senses, harmonizing with nature and living more naturally, relating to the land, experiencing our life force, freeing ourselves from excessive domestication, and finding our place and purpose in the larger universe.

The eight chapters of Part II, "Communing with Nature," take us into the actual experience of communing with the physical world of nature. This part of the book examines eight different natural realms you may connect with: earth, water, flora, fauna, biological habitats, geological features, elements of weather, and the sky. After the most important elements of each realm are discussed, you're guided into experiencing the pleasures of exploring and communing with each essential element. While being in nature always involves several of these components at once, initially focusing on each separately should enable you to engage more deeply and completely with nature's multifaceted world.

The book views and examines the natural world from a number of different vantage points, and it addresses many of the better-known and more interesting aspects of nature. But there has been no attempt to be exhaustive, which would be impossible anyway given the nearly infinite richness of nature and life. You might come up with some fruitful methods of your own for communing with nature, and it's certain that some exciting discoveries await you in the wild. Use this book as a starting point, a source of inspiration, and a resource. Then let nature take over the roles of teacher, mentor, and spiritual guide.

PART I

GETTING CLOSER TO NATURE

1

⁂

REMEMBERING
OUR ROOTS

As a society we suffer from near-amnesia regarding our nature-based past. We've almost totally lost touch with our origins. And we're no longer aware that our very existence on this planet is impossible without nature. We've created an increasingly artificial world where the newest and latest predominate, where progress and profits prevail, and where we can now live out our lives almost without venturing outside.

Our current separation from nature represents a radical break from the past; our ancestors would find our abandonment of the natural realm incomprehensible. Now that we're essentially an indoor species, walled off from the world of other lifeforms, we're divorced from the very domain that supports and sustains our lives. The changes we've seen during the past few decades have been revolutionary, but our memories are short. Many of us can no longer imagine living any other way.

Yet at the same time, we are all aware of the growing problems both inside and outside of the synthetic realm we've constructed. Signs abound that our planet is becoming increasingly unhealthy and unbalanced. Alienation, despair, and violence are widespread around the globe, and we're witnessing an explosion of environmental crises as our ecosystem continues to deteriorate. Many ecologists and other life scientists believe the long-term prognosis for human life is in doubt unless we can find ways to greatly reduce our destructive impact on the earth.

There's surely no better time than now for some self-examination as a species: to consider who and what we really are, where we may fit into the scheme of things, what could have caused us to get so out of balance with the rest of life, and how we might return to more harmonious ways of living. This chapter begins by offering a brief survey of these subjects, although they cover a vast amount of territory. By looking back at our natural origins and remembering our roots in nature, we may be able to get a better sense of what a human being is and what we need to be whole. Such an awareness could make it easier for us to start charting a more naturally fulfilling course for ourselves.

Humanity and Nature in the Recent Past

Human beings have lived in nature's embrace for all but a minute fraction of their existence here on earth, which is hard for us children of the modern world to fully grasp. Urban and suburban living are extremely recent developments. In a sense, our species is still in a state of shock from "having the earth pulled out from under us," from being seduced into adopting new and nonnatural ways of living that don't always fit us well, although they're frequently dressed in irresistibly attractive clothing. Some of these ways are clearly incompatible with our basic nature.

By all accounts our separation from nature started with the development of agriculture, which began to supersede hunter-gatherer societies some ten thousand years ago. How and why this happened remain widely disputed and are yet to be understood. A sizable portion of humanity has been on a path of growth and development ever since, using increasingly powerful technologies that have taken us further and further from nature.

The process accelerated considerably in the late eighteenth century, when industrialization began to steamroll its way across the face of the planet, transforming humanity's relationship with the land once again and intensifying the destruction of natural areas. Where nature hasn't been "harvested" or flattened, it has frequently been forgotten by the earth's increasingly busy inhabitants. The idea of regularly acknowledging our indebtedness to the natural world and giving thanks for the many gifts we receive from it, or considering other species to be our close "relations," which many indigenous peoples still do, couldn't be more alien to most of us. Few of our leaders today embody anything resembling nature-based values—although it's also true that the vast majority of our citizens do value nature, support funding for public parks, and express the belief that our air, water, and other natural resources should be protected.

Many of us in the United States have been strongly influenced by the powerful ideas of progress and the American Dream, which until recently held out the promise of perpetual material improvement for everyone. Although their roots go further back, these concepts triumphed in the twentieth century.

Many Americans still believe they can, must, and deserve to have it all, especially with respect to consumer goods. This pursuit of material gratification has unfortunately led us to trample critical ecological limits. At the same time, it has failed to make us happier or improve the quality of our lives. One of the greatest challenges we currently face is to admit the truth that our affluent lifestyles are environmentally unsustainable in the long run. We in the Western world are grabbing the lion's share of the earth's resources and rapidly using them up.

While there remains some disagreement about the seriousness of the ecological crisis, this is largely because our media haven't conveyed to us the whole complex story. Most scientists believe the potential threats posed by global warming and the deterioration of the ecosystem are serious indeed. Fortunately we still have a limited amount of time to address these issues. Perhaps the best news is that what's healthiest for the planet is healthiest for human beings and other species. We don't need to sacrifice the quality of our lives to get back on track and leave a sustainable world for future generations to enjoy, although it's true that we must find ways to limit consumption. Living more gently on the earth will actually enhance our well-being, not diminish it. And the closer we get to nature, the more easily we'll probably find ways to meet some of our deepest needs.

Looking Back to Earlier Times

While no one can accurately reconstruct our precivilized past, there are reasons to suspect that life wasn't always a never-ending struggle for our predecessors; at times they almost certainly lived in relative harmony with nature and each other, contrary to the images of harshness and brutality we've been taught were characteristic of preliterate hunter-gatherer societies. Serious threats to survival unquestionably existed (just as they do for many people in the world today), and the challenges of their day were different from ours, but it's unlikely that existence was more stressful then than it is now. Although no "conveniences" existed, populations were small and there was less competition for resources; basic necessities like food and water were often plentiful and readily available. Everyday life almost certainly required, on average, much less work than most of us do today, with enviable amounts of rest, leisure time, and play.

Even the legendary "savagery" of some earlier peoples may have been no more prevalent than such behavior is today. After all, the "civilized" twentieth century witnessed some of the worst wars, genocides, and horrific crimes ever known. And in the past, as well as now, it appears that human beings who lived in small nature-based communities and who had intimate and interactive relationships with the natural world tended to behave peacefully toward others. Such conditions may have allowed people to meet their range of needs much better than do most civilized environments, and more completely than some of us can imagine. This may be especially true regarding emotional and spiritual needs, which go unnourished for so many in today's world. Violence is extremely rare and unthinkable among those for whom life is an emotionally fulfilling and sacred experience.

It's a stretch for us to imagine earlier, simpler times, especially for the many of us who are caught up in the mad pace of modern life. Try, for a moment, to picture what it must have been like to live with largely uncluttered minds, in a quiet world, where tight schedules and linear thinking hadn't yet been invented; where there were no clocks, media, books, money, products to purchase, schools, or employment other than food-gathering, hunting, and basic tasks of communal living; and where all entertainment was self-generated.

We can never return to such a life, which seems light-years away from our current experience, nor would most of us want to. Yet some aspects of the world we've left behind contributed to the well-being and quality of life of the average person; our existence is the poorer for their absence. If we had to single out the element most missing from modern-day society, it would surely have to be the stimulating and healing presence of nature. This realm encompasses many of the blessings our ancestors were able to take for granted, most of which are in short supply today, such as fresh, clean, and fragrant air, delicious unadulterated water, pristine landscapes, and wonderfully harmonious soundscapes.

But perhaps even more important than these for human well-being—and the loss of which has caused immeasurable harm to us and indirectly to the earth—is the realm of relationships with other living things that our predecessors enjoyed. The human community wasn't isolated or separated from the larger community of life, which included every conceivable kind of creature, insect, plant, and other living being. It was normal for people to interact directly and even speak with animals and plants, as well as with rocks and other inanimate objects. During the course of these encounters gifts were sometimes offered, gratitude was expressed, and apologies were made when it proved necessary to take them for food or to meet other needs.

Alienation is unimaginable in such a world, where people have relationships with so many of the beings and objects they encounter in the course of a day or throughout a lifetime. Compare this with our often lonely ways, whether we're riding around by ourselves in air-conditioned cars or packed tight in subway trains on our way to work, attempting with a very finite number of friends and allies to navigate through seas of strangers and oceans of "unfriendly" objects and obstacles.

The Natural Lives of Our Ancestors

Imagine briefly joining a circle of your ancestors as they sat, or occasionally sang or danced, around the communal fire; or as they rested in their simple shelters, lulled to sleep by the sounds of night, which sometimes included the rhythms of heavy rains and gusty winds; or as they roamed and migrated across unbroken lands, through the vast open prairies and ancient forests that once covered much of the earth, stopping to drink from pristine streams and rivers, encountering countless other creatures large and small along the way—some of which were taken as food and others, including dangerous predators, that were avoided as best as possible. Life and death coexisted much more openly then than in our society; celebration frequently alternated with mourning for the losses of loved ones. It's important that we refrain from any temptations to romanticize their lives, even though some elements of their nature-based existence may strongly attract us. They surely knew as much about pain and suffering as we ever will.

By being a part of nature, earlier peoples were subject to many direct threats to their survival, but they were also perpetually immersed in a field of life energies that had many rich, stimulating, and healing qualities. Unless we experience it for ourselves—we can get a taste of this by spending some extended time in the wild—many of us have no idea how much the ongoing presence of other living, breathing, nonhuman beings of all shapes, characteristics, and energies can influence us, including by intensifying our sense of physical and emotional well-being. Some of us have come to believe that just as a baby has a critical need to be touched and loved, which doesn't cease when she or he becomes an adult, so do human beings have a lifelong need for contact and meaningful relationships with other-than-human beings and the natural landscape. We can only suspect what an effect meeting these forgotten needs might have on some modern-day maladies, such as our current epidemics of depression and violence.

Being an integral part of the web of life, having "friends" among other species as well as our own, and remaining permanently immersed in a positive force field of life probably made it easier for earlier peoples to deal with difficult times when they came—including coping with extreme weather, natural catastrophes, food scarcity, and conflict with others—without the benefit of the modern resources we have for dealing with such crises. And these natural sources of strength and sustenance our ancestors drew upon have by no means become extinct; they remain fully available to us today.

Our Animal Nature

No one can fail to see some of the striking similarities that exist between ourselves and our nonhuman relatives. These resemblances are one of the reasons most of us find other animals, both wild and domesticated, endlessly fascinating. While physiologically we're closest to our primate cousins, it's easy to observe aspects of ourselves in most mammals and other animals as well. Our culture doesn't exactly encourage us to acknowledge or focus on such connections, however. Most civilized societies have exaggerated the differences and claimed our superiority over other creatures for thousands of years, an attitude that has made it much easier for us to exploit animals.

The extraordinary mental and verbal abilities of human beings are unequaled in the world, but we must also acknowledge the countless ways that other creatures surpass us, especially in physical and perceptual feats. Raptors soar, pumas pounce, and other animals negotiate the roughest of terrain with perfect coordination, leaving us to look like the earth's clumsiest creatures. But any awkwardness we display is actually symptomatic of the semisedentary ways we've adopted. Observe the great poise and grace demonstrated by dancers and athletes, for example, or by people who were raised in nature-based societies.

Most of us have no desire to denigrate *Homo sapiens*, except perhaps to condemn the havoc wreaked by a small number of our species. The majority of us are happy or at least content to be human. What's called for is more respect for the myriad other creatures we share this planet with, many of whom were here long before we arrived and have an equal right to survive and thrive in the same way we all wish to in our lifetimes.

Other animals presumably remind us of our own animal nature, animal origins, and animal-like instincts. Many of us are ambivalent about these, and the culture we've been brought up in has colluded in helping us deny them. Some religions would have us reject altogether the idea that we evolved out of the animal world. All indications are that we want to and believe we're entitled to feel superior, special, and elevated in our human status. Not surprisingly, to be called an animal in our society is usually a put-down or a joke, and the epithet "animal" is often applied to people who commit despicable acts. This misuse of the word couldn't be more unfair to the animals themselves, who almost never engage in random or gratuitous violence.

On the other hand, it's interesting to note how we tend to be passionate about our pets, become excited when we encounter wildlife, and show concern for the plight of endangered animals. The popularity of zoos and TV wildlife programs reflects our intense interest in other creatures. We can easily relate to the animals "out there," although we also tend to project some of our fears onto them. What we're apparently most conflicted about is the animalness that still lives inside us. This reaction follows from what many of us learned from early childhood on: to be embarrassed or ashamed of our bodies and uncomfortable about our physical instincts and feelings, which most of us were taught to repress, redirect, or ignore.

Civilization's fears regarding a freer expression of our instincts are not without a certain justification, although we appear to have overreacted to the perceived dangers of our animal nature. No doubt we need to keep antisocial and other inappropriate impulses in check, which traditional societies are well aware of and effective in accomplishing. Repressing the *awareness* of our instincts and animal nature, however, isn't healthy. If we explore our inner world, we're likely to discover that not only are most of our instincts not dangerous or destructive, but they carry some of the seeds of our being. They convey clues and often vital information about who we really are, what we need in life, and what paths we might best take. And in the course of getting to know our deeper selves, we're sure to discover some of the most important underlying connections we have with nature and the rest of the universe.

Reflecting on Our Origins

Attempting to peer back into the earliest formative years of our species isn't easy, and the picture becomes murkier still when we move into prehuman times. It takes quite an effort of the imagination to put ourselves in the place of our tree-living primate predecessors, or going even further back, to try empathizing with the earliest life-forms.

We'll never know the entire story of the human journey from our beginnings, nor can a complete history of life on earth ever be told, although scientists will continue to search for evidence and posit theories for a long time to come. Too much of the potential evidence is irretrievable, and what can be pieced together will never explain all of the mysteries of our origins. This is one of those areas in which we must simply accept the limitations of life in our physical universe. We'll never be able to know everything, in spite of our culture's fantasies to the contrary, nor will we ever control life (at least some of us hope and pray that remains true). The sooner we accept that we live in a world of limits, the better. This isn't to say that we shouldn't aim high in life, let our imaginations fly, and even take on such seemingly impossible challenges as attempting to turn our materialistic society into a more life-enhancing one.

Contemplating our origins is never a waste of time, however, nor is studying evolution, paleontology, human prehistory, the earth sciences, and other fields that touch on life's origins; all can enrich our understanding of our roots. Perhaps the most valuable result of investigating or simply reflecting on our origins is the important reminder we receive: we're all related in some way. No species is excluded. All of life shares the same primordial roots and seeds; all of our family histories go back to the same mysterious beginnings, the same incomparable time when our planet first gave birth to life.

In the conflict-riddled modern world, our inability to find commonalities between ourselves and other human beings, especially those of different ethnic origins and beliefs, couldn't be more painfully clear. Yet equally if not more fractured are our relations with other species, which we're wiping out at frightening speed. It's sad to see how often we choose to aggress against or exploit other life-forms, rather than reach out to them; this presumably reflects our alienation, fear, and greed. While there are no easy solutions, learning to experience our connectedness with the rest of creation has the potential of transforming our perceptions of other living things from "resources" or "competition" into "community." The consequences of such an awareness can't be overestimated. It can reunite us with a legion of long-lost relatives, who may simultaneously comprise some of the most important missing parts of ourselves. Thus it's possible that awakening to our natural roots might enable us to come back into peaceful communion with life in its entirety.

2

⚭

Envisioning a More
Natural Life

THE ENDLESS BENEFITS of inviting nature into our lives are
accessible to all of us. It doesn't matter how oblivious we may
have become to the charms of the natural world during the
course of our lives or how far from our ancestors' ways we may
have strayed. We can all reconnect with our rustic roots if we
wish. We were all born with the necessary equipment, and most
of us are capable of recovering our natural receptivity. Our
underlying affinity for nature is such a fundamental part of our
makeup that it can never be entirely overridden or removed.

Ideally, relating to nature and feeling at home in the natural
world should come as naturally and instinctively to us as speaking and walking. If we respond otherwise, which many of us do,
it may be because of early familial or cultural training or the
result of inadequate exposure to nature in our younger years.
Given the other-than-natural orientation of our society, even

with the most enlightened upbringing most of us don't learn to become completely comfortable or conversant with wild nature. We need not apologize if we feel like novices.

How nature-oriented a life each of us wants to lead remains our choice alone. The range of options open to us is enormous. For some of us, simply visiting natural areas more frequently might satisfy our present needs, whereas others of us may want to completely redesign our lives to be more nature-inclusive. Whatever our particular needs and preferences, most of us can benefit from learning more about how to best approach and interact with nature's elements, including the vast array of other species we share the earth with.

Communing with nature and spending time in the wild are usually the most convenient and least complicated for those who live near natural areas and who are fortunate enough to have flexible schedules with ample free time. For others of us, especially urban or suburban dwellers who carry a heavy load of commitments and responsibilities, a bit of juggling or fancy footwork may be required to fit nature into our daily lives—but it's still something we can all achieve.

To clarify what we want and need it's sometimes helpful to ask ourselves a few questions such as: To what extent is nature lacking in my life right now? How might my relationship with nature be improved? What role would I prefer the natural world to play in my life? If I could live exactly the way I want, how natural would I choose my work and home environments to be? How much time would I spend out in wild nature each day, week, or throughout the year? What are the immediate obstacles, if any, that stand in my way of living a more nature-oriented life, and how might these barriers be circumvented or the problems resolved?

The more imaginatively and expansively we can think about our options and whatever life challenges we face, the better. There are often multiple solutions, with many more choices than we may initially recognize. Aside from trying rational problem-solving, we should allow our desires to guide us in designing a more satisfying, nature-inclusive life. And there's no harm in asking nature herself for some help by addressing these issues in her presence and allowing for her input and inspiration.

What we decide and achieve will be influenced by how strongly or passionately we feel about nature and how motivated we are to make room for her in our lives. We're sure to succeed in connecting with nature if she becomes important enough to us and we're willing to take the necessary actions. With an intense interest and longing to relate, it's almost impossible to fail. Some fears or resistances may arise along the way, especially at the start, but with sufficient motivation and intent we'll almost certainly overcome them.

We should never forget that nature lies not only in those splendid places "out there" where living things are allowed to flourish, and that serve as a personal respite for us, but she also resides fully within our own being and has the potential to blossom there when properly nurtured. We're all physical and spiritual expressions or manifestations of nature, and it's helpful to view ourselves as such. In every respect we are, after all, subject to natural processes and guided by natural forces throughout every moment of our lives, from the time of our first breath and heartbeat to our very last.

Opening Ourselves to Nature

The more psychologically and spiritually open to nature we can be, the deeper and more satisfying the experience we're likely to have in her presence. Many of us are strongly attracted to the physical beauty of the natural world, and some of us have become addicted to outdoor adventures, yet we may still maintain a certain distance between ourselves and nature. We're sure to benefit more if we're fully and emotionally available for an intimate relationship with the wild. At the same time, each of us is entitled to relate to the natural realm in whatever ways we choose and are most comfortable with. Just being there will usually be rewarding regardless of our attitudes and how we spend our time.

Fear is one of the most common obstacles that keeps us from getting close to nature. We naturally fear the unknown, which for many of us characterizes much of wild nature. Among our fears is that we'll somehow get hurt, such as taking a fall and breaking a bone, getting struck by lightning, or being attacked by a wild animal. All of these situations are extremely unlikely, and the latter, our fear of wildlife, is especially unrealistic but continues to be widely exploited by movies and other media. While it's appropriate to be careful and alert while in nature, maintaining a state of hypervigilance regarding imagined dangers is incompatible with achieving a receptive state of mind.

In preparing for outings it's wise to learn how to protect ourselves from any hazards we might encounter in the wild—and then consciously let go of our concerns and attempt to open our minds and hearts to nature's gifts as fully and positively as possible. Whenever we become aware of fears or doubts, we should briefly acknowledge them and quickly screen them for relevance. Then, after addressing any pertinent concerns that may call for follow-up, we should allow them to promptly evaporate into the ether.

We can also deal with nature-related resistances or inner hindrances, when we become aware of them, by attempting to consciously welcome nature into our hearts and psyches. Try to invite nature into your body and being, and do so in any way that seems appropriate. Address her verbally out loud if that feels right to you. If you're frequently conscious of fears elicited by nature, try spending a few minutes each day visualizing yourself resting and receiving sustenance in a safe, comfortable setting within the natural world.

By making our "internal environment" especially hospitable to nature, we invite her spirit to infuse our lives. And no matter where we are, we can carry nature around with us in the recesses of our being throughout the day. We can allow her to color and influence our perceptions of the everyday world. And by staying nature-conscious we can bring a more natural awareness to the tasks we must carry out and the problems we must solve. This basically means we're giving nature a spiritual home inside ourselves, where she rightfully has a place anyway and secretly resides even if we don't consciously acknowledge her presence. In the process, we're going to find some additional doors to communion with external nature opening to us.

Making Room for Nature

Given the hyperactive pace of modern life and our habitually overbooked schedules, coming up with enough free time for nature and fulfilling other personal needs present difficulties and frustrations for many of us. Yet the truth is that we can always find time for the things that matter most in life, no matter how overwhelming our other obligations may be. Saying we have no time for nature is almost akin to saying we have no time for food, sleep, friends, or other essentials of life. In fact, nature actually embodies and encompasses *all* of life. We slight her at our own expense; failing to find room for her can only be self-defeating for us.

Granted that since nature's status is relatively low in our society, which reflects how misguided some of our culture's values are, few if any employers will offer you "nature days" off from work so you can connect with the natural world and rebalance yourself. Perhaps someday, if we ever create an ecologically conscious world, such an idea might not seem so far-fetched.

If time is at a premium for you, it's useful to survey what you're currently doing during nonwork hours to see if you can find some underused time. Most of us can come up with an extra hour or two when we really need to. Our options might include watching less TV or cutting out other potentially time-wasting activities. Perhaps we could also try moving some of our spare-time pursuits outdoors.

Those who are retired, unemployed, self-employed, or who otherwise have the most open schedules should have the least difficulty integrating nature into weekday activities. For the rest of us, the most obvious times to visit nature are before or after work. If our workplace is near a park or other natural area, another option would be to take a nature walk at lunchtime. We might also step out for twenty minutes during our morning or afternoon coffee break; fresh air and exercise are much healthier stimulants than caffeine anyway and have longer-lasting effects.

Regardless of when we're able to find or make the time to visit nature, most of us will benefit from turning it into a daily routine. We need to give our outings high priority so they don't get bumped by competing activities on hectic days. If we wait for lulls in a busy life, we'll probably see little of the natural world. Think of your time in nature as important, precious personal time, which you can either choose to spend alone or with a companion; don't expect others to necessarily understand. Always be prepared to respond with a firm "no" to other offers, and make a strong commitment to follow through except in the event of illness, an emergency, or extreme weather. Remember that the quality of your entire day can be improved by being in nature for a relatively small amount of time. It's a minimal investment to make with multiple benefits that may include increased energy, decreased stress, and uplifted spirits.

Readying Ourselves for Reconnecting

There are also some practical things we can do prior to visiting the natural world to facilitate the process of reconnecting. One of the most basic preparations we should all make is to acquire suitable clothing and appropriate gear, if we don't already possess it. This will help assure our comfort and safety in the wild and reduce the chances that we'll experience any discomforts or other problems. What to wear and bring on an excursion into wild nature are discussed in Chapter 6.

It's also helpful to learn as much as we can about nature, which we can accomplish in numerous ways during our spare time. This can reduce the psychological distance between ourselves and the natural world and may make for more fruitful experiences once we're there. Among the options available to us are several that will be briefly discussed for the remainder of this chapter: reading and studying; visiting nature centers and environmental centers; visiting botanical gardens, zoos, and aquariums; and visiting natural history museums.

Reading and Studying

One familiar way to help initiate the process of reconnecting is by reading, which can be done outdoors, weather permitting, as well as inside. Reading and studying can increase our understanding of nature and how humanity fits into the greater scheme of things. The possible range of relevant subjects worth reading about is extensive, including literary and popular nature writings, natural history, animal behavior, anthropology, archaeology, paleontology, biology, and the other life sciences.

Many of us like to explore new territory by first reading about it, which might be one of the reasons you have this book in front of you. Reading about nature can sometimes serve as an excellent motivator to get us out to explore on our own. Read as widely as you like to complement the other things you do, but don't assume you need to master a certain amount of material or become an expert. If you prefer to minimize the reading and go directly to nature for your lessons, by all means do so.

A major pitfall of reading, especially when we rely on it too heavily, is that the process keeps us almost entirely in our heads, which is where most of us in the Western world spend too much of our time already. We need to balance reading by using the rest of our bodies as well, especially when it comes to getting to know nature. Reading alone isn't nearly enough.

Another problem is that we live in an era of extreme specialization: too many books and articles present narrow viewpoints that leave out the bigger picture. Science books typically engage the intellect, but too few of them take us emotionally or empathetically into the world of other creatures or life-forms. And if we can't relate personally to the material, such reading is less likely to bring us any closer to nature. Try to find books and articles that strongly engage your interest or excite your passion; this will make the natural world more alive and meaningful to you and may inspire you to get involved.

Visiting Nature Centers and Environmental Centers

Throughout the country are hundreds of nature and environmental centers, which serve the important purpose of educating schoolchildren and the public at large about nature, ecology, and the fragile environments we inhabit. If there's one near you, pay a visit. You'll usually find displays, exhibits, and educational information outdoors as well as indoors; you're almost certain to learn a thing or two while there.

The majority of such centers are located in relatively undeveloped areas—sometimes within state or local parks—and the larger ones often have nature or hiking trails, making it easier to explore the natural surroundings. Particular habitats are often specially maintained to attract the greatest variety of birds and wildlife, which can make such a center an excellent place to study and observe flora and fauna. Try to visit on a weekday or during off-season since it's easier to connect with the natural residents when human visitors are fewest.

Visiting Botanical Gardens, Zoos, and Aquariums

Many sizable cities have a zoo, and some have a botanical garden or a public aquarium as well. Botanical gardens are superb places to observe and learn firsthand about a myriad of local and exotic plants. Species are usually displayed both indoors and outdoors, and while their home settings aren't always duplicated, the visibility and accessibility of so many plants make examination and study extremely convenient. At a botanical garden you can meander, meditate on your place in the natural order, and let yourself be inspired by an enormous collection and often mind-boggling array of the earth's flora.

Zoos and aquariums have become somewhat controversial in modern times because of the forced captivity of their "inmates" and the cramped and unnatural conditions so many animals and aquatic creatures have had to endure. Not surprisingly, some animals have shown signs of unhappiness or mental instability. In recent years, however, major improvements have been made in living conditions at many facilities. For larger mammals in particular, the once-ubiquitous small cages have been replaced by large open habitats with space for the animals to roam more freely.

Some animal-rights activists advocate abolishing zoos and returning the animals to the wild. We must acknowledge, on the other hand, the important role zoos play in educating the public, in awakening the curiosity and interest of young children, and in helping to protect wildlife that are threatened by extinction in the wild. Given the greatly reduced natural habitat for many animals, some of them unfortunately require refuge in zoos. Everything considered, zoos seem to do much more good than harm by helping maintain public awareness of the plight of animals and ongoing threats to the world's wildlife.

Zoos remain popular with people of all ages, and for good reason. In a zoo you can come face-to-face with many creatures you would never otherwise have an opportunity to see, even if you're someone who spends a lot of time in natural areas. This is especially true for nocturnal species and those from other parts of the world. You can also safely get closer than is ordinarily possible in nature. To avoid the drawback and distraction of crowds, consider going during the week or in colder weather.

Notice how you feel and what comes to your mind when you witness other animals. Are you attracted? Curious? Repulsed? Excited? Apathetic? Empathetic? Seeing animals in the flesh usually has an emotional impact that reading about them never does. And you can learn about their behavior from observation as well as from educational displays. Remember, though, that some animals will look and behave differently in zoos than in the wild because they've been kept in tight quarters and due to the constant presence of human beings. Some will appear depressed or exhibit a much lower energy level than they would demonstrate in the natural world. Perhaps there are actions you can take to help improve the conditions of zoo animals, as well as to keep others of their species in the wild from going extinct.

Visiting Natural History Museums

If you live in or near a reasonably large city or a university town, you may be fortunate enough to have access to a natural history

museum. With its informative exhibits, displays, and films—
and impressive collections of artifacts, bones, and other remnants of earlier life—such a museum is an outstanding place to
study and learn about the history and evolution of the natural
world and humanity up to the present time. Indigenous cultures, which most of us know all too little about (since they're
largely ignored by our media and slighted by our history books),
are usually well-represented.

While much of the focus in a natural history museum is on
the past, many of the lessons to be learned are relevant to our
lives today, including our pressing ecological problems and how
we might live more in balance with the natural world. What we
witness and experience here can be stimulating and thought-
provoking, and might open some doors into nature for us.
Notice your thoughts and periodically tune into your feelings
while you're there. What touches or affects you? Does nature
speak to you in any way here? What stays with you afterward?

A museum of natural history is the perfect place to go on a
rainy, snowy, or stormy day, or anytime you're in a city, have an
hour or two to spare, and want to learn more about your origins. Here you can ponder the vast voyage life has taken over
the many thousands of millennia since our earliest single-celled
ancestors evolved into the complex, beautiful, brilliant, insight-
ful, and also strange and terribly imperfect creatures we are.

3

❦

INVITING NATURE
INDOORS

NO MATTER HOW INTENSE our interest in the natural world
might be, or how high a priority we give to spending time there,
the realities of modern life require most of us to be indoors for
the majority of our weekday hours. We may be able to duck out
for some fresh air and a taste of nature during breaks, and some
will seek lifestyles that permit a healthier mix, but for most of
us the indoor world inevitably predominates on workdays.

Fortunately, there are many things we can do while inside
that can help us stay connected with the natural world. And we
don't need to lock out nature's physical presence; dozens of plant
species and a small number of creatures can thrive indoors and
may be invited to share our spaces. We can also introduce non-
living elements of nature. Letting other beings take root in our
homes is one way to partially bridge the separation between ourselves and the larger community of life.

Shelter and Indoor Living

Living indoors is hardly a new phenomenon, although we've taken it to extraordinary lengths. Protection from the elements is one of the most basic of all human needs, and it's a requirement we share with most other animals. Shelter was sought or constructed by countless generations of our ancestors. Although earlier peoples sometimes slept out in the open, and some modern campers carry on that tradition, shelter has always been essential for survival and comfort in cold temperatures, storms, rain, snow, and other inclement weather.

As we've all heard, our prehistoric predecessors used caves and other natural shelters, camped out under rock overhangs, and more recently, bedded down inside simple huts and other structures made of rock, mud, wood, or sturdy vegetation. Shelter was something to sleep in or retreat to, not to occupy full-time. Larger dwellings were often the site of community gatherings in the evening or at night, and during the day in difficult weather, but prior to the modern era, most people were outside for the majority of their time. Food gathering, hunting, and tending crops naturally keep people outdoors, and until the industrial era, most other work and play were also done in the open air.

What's unique and unprecedented is how indoor living has become a way of life for us. Some of the consequences aren't exactly healthy, as many of us realize. We all need fresh air, exercise, exposure to full-spectrum sunlight, and other elements that aren't readily obtained indoors. And by staying inside so much, we deprive ourselves of the benefits from ongoing contact with the beauty and balance of nature.

It's important for us to remember that in spite of the obligations that keep us indoors most days, we have choices. No one needs to do all of their living, working, recreating, and entertaining inside. Some of us have become hooked on the high-tech gadgetry that fills many of our homes, on the sedentary forms of entertainment that now dominate our free time, and on indoor comforts like air-conditioning. We let these things keep us inside more than necessary, which precludes engaging in meaningful ways with our neighbors and the natural world.

"Naturalizing" Indoor Spaces

The quality and appeal of individual indoor environments vary enormously. Some homes and other spaces are comfortable and inviting, whereas many workplaces, in particular, are impersonal, uninspiring spaces that obviously haven't been designed with human needs in mind. Crowded, windowless rooms or cubicles with fluorescent lights and stagnant air are all too common, to the discomfort of those who occupy them. Aside from home and work, there are also the schools, public buildings, churches, stores, malls, movie theaters, health clubs, restaurants, and other roofed structures that we may find ourselves occupying for substantial amounts of time each week; such environments run the gamut from delightful to depressing.

How can nature help us out? Most of us are familiar with an important principle that we nevertheless frequently fail to take full advantage of: all spaces may be improved by introducing elements of the natural world. And within limits, the more we're able to add, the better. By putting plants in the windows, flowers on the tables, natural objects on your desk; choosing furniture and accessories made of natural materials; hanging pictures or paintings of natural scenes on the walls; and even introducing natural sounds via CD or tape, you're guaranteed to have a warmer, cosier, more habitable, more hospitable, more congenial place.

We're not merely speaking of making spaces more attractive and livable. What you'll gain from welcoming components of nature into your home and work space goes well beyond aesthetics and comfort. Surrounding yourself with other living things, and sometimes even just representations of them, can provide you with a source of real nourishment and sustenance, which will help you stay linked with nature when you're "stuck in captivity."

The Importance of Windows

Generally speaking, you can't have too many windows—since they serve as visual gateways to the world outside, natural and otherwise. Windows are by far the most valuable, and they assist us in staying connected with the earth, when they make accessible some basic elements of nature and the natural landscape as well as the weather. Windows that open may also be an important source of fresh air. Windowsills are naturally the perfect place for positioning plants that require sunlight.

Avoid windowless rooms as much as possible, particularly for work and other sustained use. Anyone who has "served time" in a window-free setting knows how depressing it can be to be completely cut off from any signs of nature and the world at large. Even a window that overlooks a street, or has a view of the back side of another building, or offers some other less-than-attractive perspective is usually better than no window at all. We need to relate on a regular, ongoing basis to our surroundings— to what lies beyond the walls of the buildings we occupy.

Fortunately, it's a rare window that fails to offer a view of at least something natural, even if this only amounts to a tree or two, an occasional bird, or a bit of the sky, which at times may feature the sun, moon, or stars moving ever so slowly by. Lucky are those who have windows that overlook lush greenery, a lake, or other eye-soothing scenery.

Most of us will instinctively head for a window every now and then when we're forced to remain indoors for an extended time. A window is always an appropriate location to visit, however briefly, to linger and gaze out. There's no better place to go, at least with our eyes, when taking a break from staring at a computer screen, watching TV, doing paperwork, reading, or anytime we feel restless and closed in by the walls.

Full-Spectrum Lightbulbs and Window Glass

Ordinary lightbulbs and other sources of artificial light don't provide the full spectrum of wavelengths found in natural sunlight. Reading and working under unnatural light tend to be hard on the eyes and very fatiguing. Fluorescent lights are particularly problematic as they have a barely perceptible flicker that can induce headaches and eyestrain.

Full-spectrum lightbulbs are available that offer a richer and more natural source of light for the home or workplace. While much more expensive than conventional bulbs, they last longer, are easier on the eyes, and by approximating sunlight may reduce your susceptibility to SAD (seasonal affective disorder) during

the winter months. Inadequate exposure to full-spectrum sunlight has been implicated in the depression many people suffer
at this time of year. Get the brightest lights you can find for reading and other close visual work; higher wattages (properly
shaded) will benefit you and your eyes the most.

Another way to maximize your indoor light environment is
to install full-spectrum glass in your windows. Unlike regular
glass, it allows the entire spectrum of sunlight to enter. Replac-
ing all your windows with such glass would be costly, and if you
spend enough time outdoors such an investment would be
unnecessary. But if you're indoors for most daylight hours during the colder months, when windows are closed, this could give
a natural boost to your mood and sense of well-being.

Indoor Flora and Fauna

The adaptability of different plants and animals to human environments varies enormously. Some are completely incapable of
adjusting to indoor spaces and will quickly die when trans-
planted, whereas other species can live almost anywhere when
the conditions are right and adequate food is available.

You'll naturally want to choose plants that are likely to do
well indoors or on your windowsill, which often means under
limited lighting and in a relatively small amount of soil. Consult a book on the subject for advice. Tending plants and caring
for animals are inherently rewarding for many reasons, including the physical contact as well as the relationships we develop
with them. It's good therapy for those of us who lead stressful
lives, in part because spending time with other species takes us
temporarily out of our human-centered mind-set.

Becoming personally familiar with flora or fauna by living and interacting with them has other positive consequences as well, including shifting our perceptions in a more natural direction. We can learn a lot from other beings by observing their individual characteristics or behavior, their development throughout the entire life cycle, and their differences as well as similarities. In time we may become attached to them, just as we do with people.

Aside from pets, indoor animal options are obviously limited. Having wildlife indoors is a contradiction in terms; it's usually unworkable as well as unethical. More often than not, a caged wild animal is a depressed creature with a short life expectancy. Conventional pets offer numerous pleasures, of course, including the opportunity to get to know another species, learn to communicate with it, and enjoy their company. We should keep in mind, though, that some of the domesticated animals we love are as divorced from wild nature as we are.

Pictures and Paintings of Nature

Hanging paintings and photographs of natural scenes and subjects on our walls is an easy way to help naturalize the spaces we spend time in. Don't underestimate the power of an image to affect your mind and mood. A beautiful painting, sketch, or photo will not only provide aesthetic pleasure, but usually offers an uplifting effect when the theme is a natural one. And few images are more relaxing to the eyes and mind, or calming to the nerves, or healing to the heart, than those of nature. Some of us instinctively seek them out when we're not otherwise preoccupied, especially when we feel stressed or discouraged. Such images can also remind us where we need to head—namely to nature—when "the world is too much with us" (Wordsworth).

Natural Objects, Furniture, Clothing, and Food

Using objects, sculpture, and furniture made of natural materials can not only enhance the beauty of a room but also evokes an atmosphere of nature. Such objects as rocks, stones, seashells, dried flowers, dried leaves, small branches, and spruce or pine boughs used decoratively should enliven any space. Be extremely conscientious, however, about where and how you collect such items. Never take flowers, branches, or other wild objects that aren't superabundant in nature, and heed regulations in areas where their removal is prohibited.

Chairs, tables, and other furniture or fixtures made of wood and other natural materials not only please the eye but also convey a solid, rich, and earthy feeling utterly unlike the feeling we receive from plastics and other synthetics. Be sure to find out the sources of any wooden products you want to purchase, however, and take special care to avoid buying items that come from old-growth trees, rainforests, and other endangered places or species. Rugs and other items for the home that are woven of wool, jute, and other natural fibers are similarly appealing. Such materials probably help keep us a little more nature-conscious, as they offer visual, tactile, aromatic, and possibly even energetic links to the natural environment.

Likewise, it's not surprising that cotton, wool, and silk continue to be popular fabrics for clothing, as well as for other household products, in spite of the ascendance of the synthetic age. They're attractive, their fibers are pleasing to the touch (with the exception of wool for some), and it's probably healthier to have them next to our skin. Can wearing, walking on, and sleeping under natural fibers help harmonize us with nature? Perhaps they contribute to the process, but beyond that we can only speculate. At the very least, surrounding ourselves with materials from nature can serve to remind us of the more-than-human world we come from. And natural products win extra points because they're friendlier to the environment; they're biodegradable and create less pollution in their production.

Could ingesting the living products of nature, namely unprocessed natural foods, also help connect us with the natural world in some way? Here again we can only offer hunches. The market for natural foods has grown rapidly in recent years, in part because of their nutritional value. There are certainly solid grounds for believing that unadulterated, unprocessed, and organic natural foods are superior to commercial foods that have unpronounceable ingredients. Natural foods are closer to what our hunter-gatherer ancestors ate, and they're unquestionably healthier for us than fat-and-additive-filled fast foods. It isn't far-fetched to speculate that they may positively affect our state of mind and our nature-consciousness as well.

There are now catalog companies and stores nationwide that specialize in ecologically sound, earth friendly, all-natural products. Some of the country's major environmental organizations also issue catalogs featuring nature-related items and materials. And hundreds of health-food stores carry a limited selection of such merchandise, as do an increasing number of regular stores.

Nature Sound Tapes and CDs

Just because you occupy an urban high-rise apartment or are ensconced in suburban sprawl doesn't mean you can't access some of the most appealing, exotic, and relaxing natural sounds the planet has to offer. CDs and cassette tapes are available of ocean waves, mountain streams, thunderstorms, and a host of natural environments like tropical rainforests. You can use them to create a background aural environment that is certain to give a more natural feel to your home while they're on.

Many of us who have used these recordings have found them enjoyable and beneficial, especially the relaxing and mesmerizing water sounds of streams and ocean waves. They create an extremely pleasant and soothing atmosphere that's great to work, read, or even sleep by. They're also perfect for blocking out obnoxious noises such as city sirens and screeching brakes, or suburban power mowers and leaf blowers. Such recordings will keep the sound dimension of nature within your living space and mind.

Nature Films and Videos

The immediacy and visual splendor of nature documentaries—and other films and videos that have nature themes—make them wonderful resources for anyone who's hungry to experience and learn more about the natural world. Your options obviously include watching regular nature shows on television and renting videos, as well as patronizing the occasional Hollywood movie that has a reasonably natural theme. But as you probably know, most fictional accounts tend to misrepresent nature, distort natural phenomena, and exaggerate the dangers by frequently portraying wilderness as a much nastier and more fearsome place than it really is. Look for well-done documentaries and stories that present a positive or at least relatively neutral perspective. Try to avoid the more violent and sensational nature-based movies or TV shows, which are loaded with enough negativity to sabotage your efforts to befriend nature.

Nature Slide Shows

If you're interested in photography, which is one of many possible hobbies or pastimes that can be entry points to the study or exploration of nature, chances are you'll be out and about with your camera whenever you can. Later on, back at home or elsewhere, it's often gratifying to share nature photos with appreciative friends or family. To re-create as fully as possible the visual magnificence of the natural world, try taking photos on slide film, and offer slide shows that feature your best work.

Projecting beautiful nature photos on a big screen is an especially effective way to elicit in others and yourself a desire for more contact with nature. To avoid overtaxing your audience, the usual advice is to keep presentations short, which also increases the odds that you'll be asked for an encore performance. Making a nature film is another option, but creating an interesting and watchable film requires greater talent and effort; slides are the simpler and easier way to go.

Nature Books and Magazines

The subject of reading was briefly addressed in Chapter 2, but there are some additional benefits and pleasures to consider. When we can't be there in person (and even when we can) it's rewarding to read about the wilder places and let ourselves be affected by some spectacular nature photography. Although they don't often make the bestseller lists, outstanding nature books are published every year. If you can stand a dose of inspiration, some of the writing could seduce you into reordering your priorities in a more natural direction.

No matter what our background, we all have more to learn about nature, ecology, and the myriad other species we share this planet with. The information we glean from reading could be useful on our future outings. Vicarious pleasure can also be found in reading about someone's experiences in the wild, whether it's the first-person account of a naturalist or adventurer or perhaps a fictional treatment of nature-based events. And it's a good idea to read regularly about the state of the earth and the ongoing environmental crisis, although the news isn't always encouraging. As informed citizens we're in the position to contact and influence the powers that be, who need to be pressured to make more environmentally sensitive decisions and help move our national priorities in a more earth-respecting direction.

You may also want to subscribe to a few nature and environmental magazines, if you don't already. While you're at it, consider joining and supporting some of the better-known environmental organizations and other groups that are dedicated to protecting natural areas and wildlife. Information about such groups is available on-line and elsewhere. If reading about nature appeals to you, you'll probably want to periodically peruse your bookstore, library, or the Internet for books on these subjects. And if nature becomes your passion, perhaps you'll end up with your own little home library, with immediate access to plenty of nature-related resources and inspiration for the times when you can't get out into nature often enough.

Keeping a Nature Journal

A nature journal or diary provides you with a place to regularly record observations, thoughts, and feelings regarding the natural world. Maintaining such a journal can be a good vehicle for ruminating on your experiences in nature as well as at home, and for considering the deeper questions that sometimes arise. A small journal has the advantage that it can be carried almost anywhere you go, so you can record information, insights, sightings of various species, other discoveries, and your responses to natural phenomena on the spot, as well as afterthoughts and reflections later on when you're back home.

Reflecting and Meditating on Nature

We can carry nature wherever we go, including into our home, workplace, and the other less-than-natural spaces we frequent, by keeping her in our consciousness. If we're so inclined, we can offer nature a permanent place in our minds and hearts, and we can permit her to share our everyday agendas. Simply thinking about or visualizing nature may be sufficient to bring the natural world to life inside us.

Setting aside regular time for meditation or reflection is an especially effective way of accomplishing this. While almost any form of meditation may offer potential benefits, including helping us relax and get more in touch with our inner nature, meditation can be exceptionally fruitful when we make outer nature the focus. The wild is the ideal environment, but this is also a valuable practice to carry out while at home, at work if the time and privacy are available, or in other indoor spaces.

Try meditating with the image of a natural scene or living being in your mind's eye, or while in the presence of a natural object, creature, or plant, with your eyes in soft focus. When your mind wanders, return your attention gently back to this being or landscape, without judgment. Notice your feelings and perceptions about the object or scene as they arise, without getting attached to them. Observe how they change over time. See if your sense of separation doesn't start to diminish through meditating and sharing space with this life-form. Watch for signs of feeling more connected and comfortable in its presence.

4

⁓

GETTING OUTSIDE

ONE OF THE MOST IMPORTANT IMPERATIVES for those of us who want to connect with nature is to exit as often as possible into the outdoors. We need to make every effort to regularly remove ourselves from indoor environments, indoor activities, and indoor obligations. While other options exist for those of us who are unavoidably stuck inside, the deepest, most meaningful, and most life-enhancing experiences will be enjoyed by those of us who can meet and commune with nature on her home ground.

Finding the motivation to get out isn't usually a problem; most of us are instinctively drawn outside, especially in fair weather. The urge to exit may be strongest in spring, particularly among those of us who have endured months of cold-weather confinement, but it can strike us at any time, in any season, and in any weather. Enduring eight hours or more in a stuffy office or other closed space can easily trigger such an impulse. For those of us who feel most at home outdoors, even the coldest and rainiest days aren't necessarily exempt.

Few of us spend more than a fraction of our time outside, which is one reason why some of us periodically become so stir-crazy and hungry for nature. It's why staying indoors is so difficult when the sunshine is streaming through our windows, and why we're so easily distracted by natural sounds, seduced by natural scents, and tempted by balmy temperatures, all of which invite us to leave the tasks at hand for another day.

No, most of us haven't lost our ability to respond viscerally to nature's elemental ingredients. We can be grateful that we still gravitate toward the natural, that we continue to crave clean air and open spaces, and that we long to experience and commingle with the energies of other living things. Granted, this guarantees some frustration when we're forced to remain indoors too long. We can count on nature to keep pestering us, to remind us that there are other places for us to be, and perhaps better ways for us to live as well.

Our instinct to get outside is indeed a healthy one—since some of our essential needs, which we often neglect and pay a price for ignoring, are hard to meet indoors. Taking in fresh air and sufficient amounts of oxygen, for example, is critical to our health and the optimal functioning of our bodies. Contrary to what many people imagine, air quality inside is frequently lower than it is outside, even in cities, due to chemical outgassing from furniture, rugs, and a host of other household products—combined with inadequate ventilation.

Exposure to full-spectrum sunlight is another vital human need that has received scant attention until recently. It has been overshadowed by warnings about the risks of overexposure, which doesn't negate the fact that our bodies benefit in many ways when they receive substantial doses of full-spectrum light daily.

There are also less quantifiable needs, such as for intimate contact with other living beings or to imbibe the beauty of the natural landscape. Nature, we must never forget, isn't merely an interesting or lovely place to visit; it's a primary source of our physical, psychological, and spiritual well-being.

Exiting

Our urges to get out notwithstanding, we can probably come up with ten thousand excuses for staying cooped up at home, at work, or elsewhere. Many of us have far more to do in our lives than we can ever possibly accomplish, and some of us are constantly running to try to catch up. And unless we've chosen to live a nature-based life, most of our responsibilities are likely to be indoor-oriented.

If spending time outdoors isn't already a special priority for us, we need to make it so. A minimum to strive for might be an hour or two each day, which doesn't have to be taken all at once. When we're extremely pressed for time, a short walk or a few minutes spent relaxing in our yard can still be valuable. Don't let cold or inclement weather be an excuse for staying in; just put on the appropriate clothing and go.

Some of us may find that we need to marshal some extra resolve and determination to get ourselves outside at every available opportunity, as well as to do what we can to increase our outdoor options. It's important that we respect and follow through on our urges to connect with nature in a timely way and not keep postponing or stifling them. We owe ourselves the healthy and fulfilling experiences that accompany communing with nature as much as we deserve to meet our other vital needs.

When in doubt, a good guiding principle is to consider proceeding directly to the nearest exit that leads outdoors whenever you have a few minutes to spare. If you're someone who has trouble fitting nature into your schedule, try getting in the habit of heading for the door whenever you take a break. Those of us who don't have larger blocks of free time available can still connect with nature by going out frequently for shorter stints.

Your options will naturally be affected by what's to be found directly outside your house, workplace, or school. Those of us who live next to a park or forest may only need to walk a few steps to be surrounded by nature, whereas many of us have to travel at least a few miles to reach a sizable natural area. But we don't need wilderness to commune with nature, and what's available outside our door will sometimes suffice. Suburbanites are likely to have a lawn with some trees, bushes, and a small selection of wildlife nearby. Most city dwellers have a minimum of a few trees on the street, some birds on the windowsill, and blue sky overhead.

Whenever you're outside and not on your way somewhere or otherwise preoccupied, an appropriate first step is to get off the sidewalk or pavement and onto some grass or bare ground. If you live in a city you may have to find a park for this, although there are even limited ways of communing with nature with asphalt or concrete under your feet. Sidewalks and roads prove useful when you have to get somewhere, but for the rest of the time you're much better off walking, standing, sitting, playing, and doing practically everything else on "unimproved earth."

Once you're on the ground, or the closest facsimile you can find, and particularly if you've just emerged from a stint of stressful work or are otherwise in a nonnatural mind-set, it's helpful to stop and take some slow, deep breaths. You can do this with your eyes open or closed. An advantage of closing them is that they'll get a bit of needed rest, which also helps you disconnect from the day's activities. Breathing deeply will furnish you with ample doses of fresh air, which can revive or energize you and also fosters letting go of stress. Use restraint, however, if the air isn't reasonably clean. You may want to do a bit of stretching to loosen up your body, especially if you've been sitting for a while. The next chapter will discuss further the subject of how to ground and connect yourself to the earth.

If you've had your eyes closed, open them now. Using minimal effort, gradually and gently scan the landscape, surveying everything within sight, and especially allowing any living things to enter your visual field and awareness. Try to see them freshly; imagine this is the first time you've ever witnessed these flora and fauna. Now lift your eyes to take in the sky as well. Then notice your mood, your level of relaxation, and whether you feel in any way connected with the land and life-forms before you. This is one of many practices you can do upon exiting from a building when you have a few minutes to spare—to help you disengage from the workaday world and bring nature and the living landscape fully into your consciousness.

If you're outside with some free time and no particular agenda, you have a nearly infinite number of choices open to you. There will often be something in particular you want to do, which could include some tasks to be accomplished. Maybe you've brought some work or reading along with you, and your next step may be to find a comfortable spot to sit, perhaps using a favorite tree as a backrest. Or you could be itching to take a long walk and do a bit of exploring. Or you might just want to poke around the yard, or simply stay put.

If you have no pressing goals or chores to undertake, and you feel adventurous, see if you can go out with no preconceived intention or goal whatsoever. Follow the lead of whatever feeling, impulse, or inclination may emerge, which could result in some interesting and fruitful experiences in nature. Before heading back inside, briefly note what's changed for you, including your state of mind and emotions.

Spending Time in the Yard

No matter how limited it may be in size or attractiveness, almost any lawn or unpaved yard can serve as an entry point to nature. The yard is a transitional zone linking the human and natural worlds, although most lawns lean heavily toward the human. Assuming you do have a yard or bit of open ground outside your house, and it's a reasonably congenial and quiet space, take advantage of it whenever you can.

Instead of curling up indoors in your favorite chair to read, do it outside in a lawn chair, sitting in the grass, or reclining under a shady tree, weather and temperature permitting. You could bring other transportable activities and sedentary tasks outdoors as well, such as light paperwork and writing. Other options might include meditating, resting, and napping.

Whenever you glance up from whatever you're doing or not doing, you'll usually find green grass, bushes, trees, clouds, open sky, and other agreeable nonlinear shapes and forms to rest your eyes on or examine. Chances are you'll look up from any activity much more often than when you're working or reading indoors. Shifting your visual focus frequently reduces your likelihood of getting eyestrain or tiring quickly of close-up work. You'll also be in a position to observe the constant comings and goings of birds, squirrels, chipmunks, and other critters that may live in your yard or frequent the neighborhood, including bees, grasshoppers, and other insects. You may not be endeared to every such neighbor, especially the tiny ones that bite, but in time you may find that peaceful coexistence is possible.

Whenever you're not busy or are taking a break, try to get to know the flora and fauna that make your yard their home. Examine especially any trees, bushes, and other plants that grow there. Don't hesitate to get down on your hands and knees for a closer look at smaller species. It's helpful to wear casual clothes so you won't mind getting a little dirty. See how many of the things you encounter you can identify, using field books when necessary. Observe the birds that nest in your trees as well as those that pass through at different times of year, and keep an eye out for the mammals that inhabit your area. Can you hear any nocturnal creatures from your bedroom window?

Having a Bird Feeder, Birdhouses, and Birdbath

A sure way to get to know birds better is to attract them to your backyard or windows with a feeder, a birdhouse or two, and a birdbath. You'll greatly increase your awareness of birds of all kinds and inevitably learn more about them when they're feeding and congregating right outside your window. Unlike in the woods, you won't need binoculars to identify different species and observe their behavior. Since so many of them migrate, what you'll see will vary enormously from one time of year to another. It's an interesting show that keeps changing.

Bird habitat is endangered in many parts of the world, and populations of some species have been plummeting, so we may be helping them out by providing food and friendly habitats. In return we get to enjoy the presence of these extraordinarily beautiful, melodic, soaring, and inspiring feathered vertebrates in our yards, trees, and airspaces. As with other living things, they bring their own endless energies to the smorgasbord of life.

It's possible to attract wild animals as well by providing food for them, but this is a more questionable and probably unwise practice, except in extreme conditions where their survival is at risk. The problem with feeding wildlife is that we may create a dependency on our handouts; when we're not around, the animals may suffer or cause problems for our neighbors. Feeding them can also result in a local population explosion, which may adversely affect the well-being of other species. The best thing we can do for most wildlife is to try to assure that their natural food sources remain abundant.

Gardening

Gardening allows us to actively participate in natural processes right outside our homes, which is one of the reasons why it's such a popular pastime. You can garden on any scale, from tending an inconspicuous little plot to stewarding an expansive tract. For some gardeners the primary purpose is to provide food for the table, but a major incentive for many is the enjoyment of helping to bring into creation an extraordinary array of plants and flowers. Much of the reward is the activity itself.

Gardening allows you to have intimate hands-on contact with soil and vegetation, and offers exercise through the necessary digging, hoeing, planting, and watering. Like farmers, gardeners are inclined to become more observant and aware of seasonal progressions and temperature changes, and inevitably get to know the needs of individual species. One of the greatest satisfactions is witnessing and guiding the transformation of seemingly lifeless bulbs and seeds into an endless variety of vibrant plants, each with its own unique properties, some of which bloom in a shower of beauty.

What we learn from gardening differs in some respects from what we'll glean from interacting with wild plants in the natural world, but it can nevertheless provide a wonderful entry point into a deeper appreciation and understanding of the life process. In getting close to floral life and being inspired by it, our relationship with nature can only deepen.

Doing Outdoor Chores

Those of us with houses and yards to take care of have chores awaiting us throughout the year, including maintaining the lawn, cleaning windows, occasionally repainting the house, fixing the roof, and shoveling snow. Some busy people now farm out such activities to others, but doing outdoor chores can be surprisingly pleasurable if we go about them in the right way. And they give us additional opportunities to be outside.

The best way to go about accomplishing such chores is to do everything at a leisurely, unrushed pace, enjoying the rhythmic movements of the activity and stopping often to watch the birds, listen to the crickets, appreciate the fresh air, and feel the sun's warm caress. Going low-tech is most gratifying; do your best to eliminate any noisy, nerve-jarring machinery, which also means you'll get more exercise. Yes, it's still very possible to mow and rake the lawn by hand, and you'll feel an unequaled sense of satisfaction in the process. Another old-fashioned and simple pleasure you can avail yourself of is to forgo the dryer and hang your washed clothing out on a clothesline.

It's worth questioning, incidently, how much sense it makes to spend a lot of time and money maintaining the lawn; having a perfect lawn is one of America's stranger obsessions. A neatly trimmed lawn isn't exactly a natural or biologically rich environment, and the widespread use of chemical herbicides moves lawn care into the realm of ecologically harmful practices. Consider letting your lawn go to seed and become a meadow by not cutting it. This will allow the area to become more biologically diverse by attracting a much wider and more interesting range of flora and fauna. Unfortunately, failing to maintain your lawn is illegal in some towns and suburbs. Whatever you do, refrain from using herbicides and pesticides, which pollute local waters, enter the food chain, and eventually end up in our own bodies.

Having Picnics, Barbecues, and Outdoor Social Events

Food always seems to taste better outdoors, and having picnics, barbecues, and even regular meals outside is almost always a good idea. The same holds true for parties, gatherings, and other social events. Everyone can use the fresh air, and no one becomes satiated with greenery and other natural elements. It's also easy to observe how the energy levels and moods of friends and family members seem to rise when outdoors, as tensions simultaneously tend to drop away.

We could even speculate that family and marital problems might be diminished if people would only spend more time together outdoors. We all need a modicum of physical and psychological room, and indoor living often means a deficiency of such space, especially for those who share small houses or apartments. A great deal more room is available outside, much more than we need. And we experience an especially delicious sense of spaciousness when we visit natural areas.

Encouraging Kids to Play Outside

Children love to be outdoors and particularly enjoy visiting the natural world. They need to be exposed to nature as often as possible; kids are kept indoors at home and school far too much for their own good. There's no better prescription for curing restlessness or rambunctiousness than to let them run free in the yard or to play in a nearby park or playground. We should take them with us on our outings into the wild as well.

Human beings benefit from contact with nature from the day of their birth on. If children are allowed to spend ample time outdoors, they're bound to feel at ease and at home in natural surroundings. In the long run they'll probably develop a lasting appreciation and love for nature, and learn to care about other living things. We need nothing more now than citizens with a committed concern for the earth, who have had instilled in them a deep appreciation for the natural world.

Some parents are excessively concerned about safety—and keep their children from climbing trees, chasing each other through woodlands, or otherwise playing in nature for fear they'll get hurt. We can most strongly show our concern for their long-term well-being by trusting and encouraging kids to play outdoors, including in natural settings, with proper supervision until they're old enough to be self-sufficient.

Enjoying Outdoor Exercise

Many of us join gyms and health clubs, sometimes paying substantial sums of money for annual memberships. Health clubs and gyms have many attractions and advantages, including impressive facilities with swimming pools, indoor tracks, and exercise machines of every possible description. Yet outdoors we can get all the exercise we need for absolutely free.

Running, jogging, and walking, for example, are extremely healthy activities that we can enjoy in the neighborhood or at the nearest park or natural area. Aside from the zero cost and the wonderful workout such activities give us, the benefits include being able to breathe fresh air, enjoy some seminatural scenery, and make our own route across the local landscape. In contrast, running in a gym or on a small indoor track sometimes means being in a stuffy building where there may even be a risk of colliding with others.

Bicycling is another activity that provides a great workout if we do it vigorously, especially in hilly terrain. Aside from cycling for recreational purposes, we can slip some extra exercise into our daily routine by commuting to work or school on our bike, which also saves us bus or train fare or gas costs and reduces our contribution to air pollution. Similarly, we should consider walking or riding our bike to get to the store, rather than taking the car, which gives us another bit of exercise while running an errand. Additional possibilities for outdoor exercise include in-line skating and ice skating. Chapter 6 will discuss a number of other outdoor recreational activities that can be done in the natural world, including hiking, canoeing, kayaking, and cross-country skiing.

Visiting Local Parks and Recreation Areas

Most of us live reasonably close to a park or recreation area. If we're in a city, we're probably within walking distance of at least a small park or two. Apartment-dwellers, or those who otherwise don't have access to a yard, will probably find it worthwhile to visit the local park as frequently as possible; every day certainly isn't too often, especially if it's in a convenient location.

Small city and suburban parks have their limitations. They're often landscaped with nonnative species and may present a thoroughly domesticated appearance; some only offer a narrow slice or suggestion of the richness and diversity of the natural world. Yet they remain invaluable enclaves amid suburban commercial strips and urban canyons, where a variety of species can nevertheless be found, including many migrating birds. If you have kids, bring them along whenever possible to share a taste of nature with you.

Taking Nature Walks in the Neighborhood

Taking a morning or evening walk—or an afternoon walk on weekends—is a great way to make a daily connection with nature. Not all of us are so lucky that we can walk directly into the natural world from our doorstep. Some of us may need to take public transportation or get in our cars to find a reasonably quiet, safe, and natural place to walk. However, most rural areas and the majority of towns, small cities, and other semideveloped areas offer access to elements of nature on foot. Best for walking are lightly traveled paths, trails, sidewalks, or roads where the sounds of civilization are relatively muted.

Walking on sidewalks or alongside roads isn't exactly a substitute for following nature trails or other wild paths in the woods. But when the latter aren't readily available, roads and sidewalks will often do. Nature still has relatively free reign in some partially developed areas where public parks don't exist. Many elements of the natural world may still be visible from paved pathways, and there's the ever-present possibility of encountering wildlife, especially at dawn or dusk.

Wherever you walk and however far you go, try to stay nature-minded. Notice how many species seem to thrive amid development. At the same time, others that were here in the past are probably gone because of their inability to adapt to the pollution, noise, and other pressures of civilization. Stop and examine any vegetation you're unfamiliar with or that otherwise attracts your attention. Appreciate the extent to which the landscape is enhanced by the presence of so many living things.

5

⟡

GROUNDING OURSELVES

NOTHING IS MORE HELPFUL in connecting with nature than making direct contact with the earth. Something important happens when we physically touch the ground—when we plant our feet on the soil, sit in the sand, or stretch out in the grass, and when we stride across the natural landscape. It's almost like making physical contact with another being; the effect can be deeply reassuring if we're receptive to it. An unmeasurable but unmistakable energy flows into our bodies from the earth, which supports us in a way no other surface can.

Many of us move our bodies hurriedly and absentmindedly through the world as if we were oblivious to what's around us. We remain absorbed in our thoughts or feelings, paying little attention to the messages of our senses and instincts, and unresponsive to the more subtle feedback from our surroundings. How often do we stop, especially when traversing wild and open ground, and really listen, look, smell, and feel the earth beneath our feet? Standing still for as little as a few minutes may feel like an eternity to those who have trouble slowing down, but the effect can also be extremely peaceful. And it becomes easier, increasingly pleasurable, and even addictive the more we do it.

By simply standing on the earth we ground ourselves. And if ever there were people who needed grounding, it's us frazzled citizens of the twenty-first century, who live so much in our heads and tend to spend more time in front of computers and video screens than face-to-face with other people or nature. A sense of security comes from simply feeling our weight fully on the ground, held there by the force of gravity—the living matter of our bodies temporarily linked to the organic earth. Standing or sitting on a floor simply isn't the same.

Although our planet constantly turns, shifts, and changes, and it's the site of severe storms as well as natural catastrophes—some of which are intensified by our civilization's dramatic impacts on the earth—it remains the reliable foundation and wellspring of life. It's covered, of course, by a relatively thin protective layer of atmosphere that allows us to breathe and live. For native peoples the earth's surface is a sacred landscape, which makes it unthinkable to treat her with anything other than the greatest respect and reverence.

Touching the earth can help us recharge our physical, emotional, and spiritual batteries; it sometimes feels like we're connecting with a vital current of life energy. Merely placing our body on an undisturbed patch of the planet's surface for a time can result in a noticeable boost of energy and morale. We may also observe our mind starting to quiet down, our pulse slowing (assuming we're resting), and any anxieties beginning to lessen. Unless we're already a nervous wreck, it's difficult to stay stressed-out for long while we're in contact with the earth.

Most of us spend the bulk of our time inside buildings, separated from the ground by thick layers of concrete, steel, and other dense materials, which form a nearly impenetrable barrier to the earth's energies. Some of us live in high-rise buildings, perched in apartments many stories above the street. Even the ground floor may be some distance above the actual soil, which can be dozens of feet below the street in a large city. A suburban house may offer easy access to a yard, but the closest place to the earth indoors is probably the cement floor of the basement. It's interesting to speculate whether some of the anxieties experienced by so many modern people might be caused or at least exacerbated by being perpetually cut off from the earth.

Stop for a moment to consider where you are in relation to the planet's surface right now. Assuming you're not in your yard or out in nature, you might be anywhere from a few to several hundred feet above the earth, or you could be below ground-level. If you're someone who spends much of your time in multi-storied buildings, try making a mental note of your location relative to the ground a few times each day. This won't always be easy to do inside larger structures that include windowless rooms. But it's a little like verifying your position on a map; it's easier to stay oriented in the world and remain grounded throughout the day when you can identify your position relative to the earth.

In cities and villages most of the walking we do outdoors is on sidewalks. Often our only other option is to walk in the street or along the shoulder of a road. Consider avoiding paved surfaces, however, whenever it's possible to walk directly on bare or grassy ground, as is usually found in a park, and you're not in a hurry to get somewhere. Circumstances and conditions per-

mitting, take off your shoes and socks, which will let you actually feel the earth with your bare feet. Footwear not only keep
our feet confined but also severely restrict their sensory input.
On the other hand, most of us necessarily depend on shoes and
boots to protect our soft civilized feet, although the latter would
probably be tough enough to deal with rough ground if we grew
up in the wild. Leave the footwear on if and when you must.
They may get in the way a bit, but they won't keep you from
grounding yourself or getting to know the earth's surface.

Standing

Whenever you've recently disembarked from a building,
whether it's your house, apartment building, or the office complex you work in, once you've reached a suitable patch of
unpaved ground it's time to shift mental gears. Breathe deeply
and start to temporarily let go of the day's business and whatever
work may still await you. Try being as fully present to the earth
as possible. You'll gain a lot more in an attentive state of mind
than a distracted one; but go easy on yourself if you're tired.
There are times when we need to give ourselves permission to
totally relax, disengage, and even space out.

   If you've been rushing around all day or simply working
hard, there's no better place than the natural world to slow down
or stop and rest. But it could also be the case that you've been sitting for too long, have a surplus of nervous energy to expel, and
crave some vigorous exercise. You're welcome to act immediately
on that impulse to move. Perhaps you already have a regular
walking, hiking, running, or cycling routine, and you're itching
to be on your way.

But before starting, try standing still for at least a few moments once you've made contact with the earth. The more time you spend for this, the better. Notice any sensations in your body while taking some slow, deep breaths. What does the earth feel like underfoot? Are you aware of any energies flowing into your body? What's pleasurable, if anything, about being here in this way? Can you enjoy the passage of time without having to glance at your watch? Experience the solidity of your body as it rests on the earth. If you're finding it hard to keep still or to maintain your balance, do you know why? Stay in this position as long as you're comfortable there.

Standing is also one of the best stances for observing, sensing, and taking in other information about the world around us. While walking we inevitably fail to see much of what's along the way, especially in nature. And the faster we go, the more we're likely to miss. Those who enjoy keeping an aerobic pace, which is extremely beneficial physically, pay a price for it. Most of the wildlife within earshot will flee quickly from the sounds of our footsteps. Animal sightings are rare among fast walkers who don't choose to periodically slow down, or stop and stand, or sit quietly. When we speed along, we also miss thousands of small and unobtrusive plants, flowers, other living things, and interesting inanimate objects.

Walking

For getting around, however, absolutely nothing beats walking. It's the perfect form of self-propelled transportation for human beings, and it's one of the best ways to go when we want to see the natural world up close and in detail. It's also ideal for exercise; our bodies couldn't have been better designed for it. Taking daily walks in nature is one of the healthiest of habits we can develop. Few things are more satisfying than the feeling of physical fulfillment and contentment that accompany a walk in the wild, whether it's leisurely or brisk.

Most of the everyday walking we do on sidewalks and floors is so routine and unvaried that we're usually completely on automatic pilot. Almost everything underfoot in civilization is flat and predictable. We may look or glance down at our feet, but more often we gaze ahead or off to the side. There's little we need to look out for besides an occasional obstacle.

Walking on the earth in natural surroundings feels like a very different activity, especially in hilly or bumpy terrain. Because of the ground's irregularities we're forced to be more alert and pay constant attention. If we fail to do so we risk tripping and falling. The length of our stride may vary depending on what's underfoot, so one step is sometimes different from the last one. We may go over or around rocks, tree roots, and other obstacles, and ascend or descend hills; the ground can be smooth or rough, soft or hard, dry or wet.

Slow walking is best for communing with nature and the environment and for staying grounded on the earth. This doesn't mean you can't walk faster when you want to, especially if it feels like a more natural pace for you. But it's worth trying to slow down at times, particularly when you want to tune in to the earth or become more aware of your feelings and "inner ecology."

More important than your pace, however, is the amount of consciousness you bring to your walking. You'll probably feel closer to nature and more in touch with the earth during a fast walk that's done with heightened, vigilant awareness than during a leisurely walk that's done in a spaced-out state, lost in your thoughts or in music from headphones. Try to be as receptive as possible with your entire body and being, and listen carefully to the reports your senses deliver as you proceed.

Sitting

Even avid fitness walkers and long-distance hikers need to rest their bodies. And while some people believe chairs have their charms (civilization would presumably be at a loss without them), there's really no better place in the world to sit than directly on the earth, whether in the grass, on a slab of rock, in some sand, or on any other natural surface. Most of us will instinctively seek out a comfortable spot to sit if we can find one, but don't let rough and rocky ground deter you from resting. You could also bring along a small piece of foam or an inflatable pillow to sit on if you like, although most of us manage without such aids.

Sitting is the posture for quietly and reflectively taking in the world. If we place ourselves strategically to blend in with the background, this will reduce our chances of being seen by wildlife and increase the probability that they'll happen upon us or pass by unaware of our presence. If we feel at home in nature, and are comfortable relaxing without having anything in particular to do, time will probably go quickly; it's more likely to drag if we're impatient and intolerant of inactivity.

If you're an experienced meditator, you'll probably want to try meditating in nature if you haven't already done so. Sit in a cross-legged position or rest your back against a tree or a boulder. If you've been following a well-traveled trail, you may want to get off the path for some relative quiet and privacy.

If you've never meditated before, simply try sitting in a comfortable position, closing your eyes, and following your breathing. Don't worry if your mind is busy or agitated; simply let thoughts come and go without getting attached to them. Don't try to shut out the sounds and scents of nature; allow them full entry into your consciousness. You may want to meditate or gently focus on them as well. Feel your buttocks resting on the earth as you sit, and notice any other sensations and feelings that arise in your body.

Even if you don't choose to formally meditate, simply being in nature offers some of the benefits of meditation, especially if you're willing to sit quietly. If you stay with it long enough, you may find yourself in a state of deep relaxation and equanimity, although at first many of us are likely to become intensely aware of inner turmoil amid the placid surroundings. It's wise to avoid judgments and expectations about what happens. Another advantage of such a practice is that tuning into the earth is easiest when you sit relatively still. Maintaining this contact for a period of time could increase your sense of spiritual connectedness with the planet.

Lying Down

Grass, sand, piles of fallen leaves, beds of pine needles, and other soft, natural surfaces often invite us to stretch out and rest. The same sometimes holds true for large slabs of rock scattered alongside streams or waterfalls—especially when they're sun-drenched—as well as contoured rock surfaces along open cliffs, canyon rims, and mountaintops, where dreamy vistas are typically available. There's no way to get closer to the earth than by lying directly on it.

Consider giving in to any impulses to recline in a "natural bed"—after first quickly surveying the area to confirm that no potential hazards are present, such as poison ivy or sharp objects. If you feel sleepy, let yourself doze off, assuming the location seems like a safe and appropriate place to sleep. When you later awaken, take note of any dreams you remember; sometimes they may include unusually vivid and striking imagery. Consider how rested you feel afterward.

More often than not, taking a nap in nature is a wonderfully refreshing experience, especially after a stint of good exercise. Some of us find sleeping directly on the earth to be more restful than anywhere else in the world and consistently superior to sleeping indoors. One of the great pleasures of camping out can be the superb quality of the sleep, although those who aren't entirely at home in the natural environment may find it to be otherwise at first. It can take at least a few nights to get used to a world so different from our bedrooms, with so many unfamiliar night sounds, some emitted by creatures that are roaming about. To sleep comfortably for the night it's also important to find a relatively smooth and level spot to camp on, use a reasonably thick foam pad for comfort, and have a warm and cozy sleeping bag.

Lying down isn't only for sleeping, though. We can stretch out on the ground in the local park—assuming there aren't "keep off the grass" signs—or in our backyard, or at the beach. Consider the millions of people who love sitting or lying in sand at the shore. This isn't exclusively about sunbathing, swimming, and listening to the pounding waves; it's also about the pleasures of sitting, reclining, or lying on some warm earth.

Lying down is also the perfect position for observing the inverted bowl of the sky and watching the clouds roll by or gazing at the stars at night. In woodsy areas the ground is a good vantage point for studying the canopy of trees overhead and watching the goings-on of birds, squirrels, and other tree-dwellers. Looking up from the ground also gives us a different perspective of the world at large. It can be a suitable stance for engaging in a session of problem-solving, pondering issues, and sorting through our thoughts and feelings.

Ultimately, the more time we spend in physical contact with the surface of the planet, the more grounded we're likely to become. Some of the possible positive results that could follow over time include finding our thoughts and feelings becoming less scattered and disconnected, our sense of self becoming more solid, and life becoming more reality-based and balanced. Connecting regularly with the earth may contribute some of the meaning and spiritual rootedness that many of us seek and sorely need.

6

❧

ENTERING THE
NATURAL WORLD

WHENEVER TIME AND CIRCUMSTANCES ALLOW, there's no better place for us to head than the nearest park, forest, preserve, refuge, reservation, sanctuary, or other natural area—and the larger and more pristine, the better. If possible, it should be a place where we can totally immerse ourselves in nature, where relatively few other people are present, and where the sounds of traffic and other man-made noises are absent or at least distant.

To visit an unspoiled part of the natural world is to practically enter another universe. Although there will usually be signs of past or present human influence, here other beings greatly outnumber humans, almost nothing is artificial, and the guiding assumptions of civilization don't hold sway. Here life is permitted to express itself with wild abandon, and all who enter are immersed in a sea of healing energies.

The benefits multiply the longer we stay. Remaining for several hours or more, which is admittedly a lot of time for busy people to manage, can reap incredible rewards if we're willing to do it regularly—preferably at least once a week. For most of us this will mean on weekends. Not all of us are able to make such a commitment, but as with so many other things, if something means enough to us we usually can find a way to make it happen.

Shorter visits have their value as well, especially when combined with longer outings on weekends. The ideal is to spend some time in nature each and every day, which is usually most feasible for those who live near undeveloped areas. How many of us can't fit at least a short nature walk into their daily schedule?

Those who don't have convenient access to wilder places need to take advantage of what's available, including semideveloped urban or suburban parks. We don't need a pristine wilderness to tune into nature and commune with her. And while it's worth periodically traveling to larger natural areas, we're also well-served by maintaining a connection with nature close to home.

When we get in the habit of daily or regular outings, we're likely to find the natural world becoming a vital refuge for us, a place we greatly look forward to visiting each time. Rather than feeling like an obligation to be fulfilled, communing with nature can come to be a treasured highlight of our week. And once we're hooked, everyday life will feel incomplete without it.

Nature-Based Recreation

There are many reasons why we visit the natural world, and there's an almost unlimited number of things we can do while we're there. For millions of people the primary attraction and motivation is to engage in such recreational activities as hiking, canoeing, kayaking, rafting, cycling, horseback riding, cross-country skiing, or snowshoeing. Being in nature is inevitably part of the appeal, but the primary focus is often on the activity itself.

Outdoor activities may be pursued in many different ways, and most forms of recreation are inherently enjoyable no matter how we go about them. Among our choices is how physically ambitious we want to be. The degree of difficulty can range from easy and leisurely to extremely strenuous and challenging. While it's helpful to be in decent shape, contrary to what many people imagine you don't have to be especially athletic or fit to engage in most recreational activities. It's only important that you stay within the limits of your ability. Almost any pursuit is taxing if you attempt to do it at great intensity for hours on end, as in a marathon. It's infinitely easier, on the other hand, if you go slowly, take frequent breaks, and stop when you're tired.

In the media and elsewhere, outdoor recreational activities are commonly referred to as sports. A small number of participants practice them as competitive sports, but many more engage in these activities for altogether different purposes: to connect with nature, unwind from everyday stresses, get some exercise, add a little adventure to life, and have fun. We may enjoy challenging ourselves physically as well, but if we take it to an extreme or are obsessively goal-oriented about it, outdoor recreation won't bring us close to nature. We're most likely to hear nature's voice when we refrain from overly identifying with or being possessed by any one activity.

Walking and Hiking

Walking has already been briefly discussed, but more can be said about walking in the natural world. In spite of all the advertising hype that promotes modern motorized recreation, going on foot is still one of the best and most popular ways to enter and explore nature. There's no better way to get to know the natural world intimately, since our feet can take us almost anywhere we want to go and at a pace that allows us to see the details of our surroundings and examine them as closely as we wish. It's the perfect self-propelled activity.

A walk can be short or long, easy or strenuous, leisurely or aerobic. Walking is something we can do entirely on our own terms and at our own pace. There are no skills we have to master and no risks other than the possibility of stumbling and falling, which could happen just as easily at home as in the woods. Few things feel more physically right to most of us than the natural movement of our body as we walk. We seem to belong on foot.

Walking can become a meditation if we want. Slow walking is most conducive to a meditative state of mind. Rather than focus on our breath, we can observe in a relaxed, unattached way the movement of our feet or the ground as it passes beneath us. Once in a while try experimenting with walking in slow motion, as slowly as you possibly can; see if this doesn't decelerate your nervous system and put you in a more peaceful state.

When we walk for longer distances over rocky, rugged, or any other natural terrain, the activity is usually called hiking. Most of us hike in public parks and forests, following marked trails designated for this purpose. Such trails often lead to scenic places like waterfalls, lakes, and mountaintops. Taking a hike allows us to survey the natural landscape, visit relatively remote areas, and get a great workout. En route we can commune with nature to our heart's content.

In the course of taking a hike there's sometimes a tendency to go on automatic pilot or cruise control, letting our legs carry us forward while we become lost in our thoughts or hypnotized by the flow of repetitive movement. This can be pleasurable, but it won't help us connect with nature. What's more fruitful is to keep our senses focused on the land as it moves under us and to tune into the multitude of messages—some strong, others subtle—that are transmitted by the earth's endlessly stimulating assortment of other living things.

It's also worthwhile to take a long break every now and then, not only to rest, but to ground ourselves, make some extended contact with a particular locale, and attempt to commune with the life there. It's this kind of connecting that often makes a walk or hike extra special and occasionally even magical. For a much more extensive treatment of nature walking and hiking, including detailed listings of the most suitable places to enjoy these activities in all fifty states, see my books *The Essential Guide to Nature Walking in the United States* and *The Essential Guide to Hiking in the United States*.

Canoeing, Kayaking, and Rafting

Natural waterways are extremely attractive to most of us and navigating them can be fun, so it's not surprising that canoeing, kayaking, and rafting are so popular. Both kayaking and canoeing originated centuries ago among indigenous peoples as means of water travel, and they've been successfully adapted to modern recreational purposes. In a canoe or kayak you can gently paddle around a scenic lake or down a slow-moving stream. Or if you're more adventurous, you can take on the challenges of riding some churning whitewater on a wild river, which will surely quicken your pulse. This may also be done in a raft, making for an especially exciting group activity. Sea kayaking is another option that can be enjoyed along coastal areas.

Almost anyone can pick up basic canoeing or kayaking skills with a bit of instruction, and there's no harm in fooling around on your own in a small lake or pond. Advanced whitewater technique, however, naturally takes much more time to acquire. It's best to learn what you need to know from a recognized school or a certified instructor, and you should go with a group or guide whenever whitewater is involved. If you have limited expertise and want to kayak or canoe on your own or with friends, limit yourself to lakes, ponds, and flatwater rivers.

Floating down a river can be one of life's most refreshing and exhilarating experiences, enveloped as you are in a liquid universe, negotiating rapids, using skill and sometimes muscle-power to stay on course, and communing with the current as it carries you along to your destination. The easier and more peaceful way of connecting with the natural world of water is to paddle out onto a placid lake and float for a few hours. If you can, choose one where motorized craft are prohibited, since motorboats and jet skis are incompatible with the quiet enjoyment of nature. Your options include watching waterbirds fishing or insects circling, doing some fishing of your own, looking for wildlife arriving at the shore to drink, taking a swim, napping, reading, meditating, or simply soaking in the rippling, reflecting, shimmering, sunlit or moonlit water.

Cross-Country Skiing and Snowshoeing

Too many of us stay home in winter because of the cold and snow, and our need for nature goes totally unfulfilled until spring. Combined with the insufficient sunlight received, this helps explain why so many people get depressed in winter. Those who take up cold-weather activities, in contrast, tend to find their spirits higher and their attitudes improved. Granted, the natural world doesn't initially seem as inviting at this time of year, but with the right clothing and gear we can find communing with nature in winter as memorable as in any other season.

Both cross-country skiing and snowshoeing are ancient activities that were developed by indigenous peoples for effective travel through snow. In the modern era they've been transformed into recreational activities that multiply the possibilities for nature exploration and fun in winter.

On cross-country skis you can glide across flat ground and ski both uphill and downhill. Contrary to downhill skiing, cross-country offers a terrific workout if you do it aerobically, but you can also enjoy it in an easier, gentler way, shuffling along and stopping as often as you want. It does take some time to learn, but cross-country skiing tends to be fun the first time out. And it's a great deal safer and less expensive than downhill skiing.

Snowshoes let you walk on top of the snow without sinking in much. They keep you afloat because of their large surface area.

In snowshoes you can go almost anywhere in the snow, no matter how deep it is and whether or not there's a trail. You don't need any instruction; it's just like learning to walk in giant shoes that feel a bit clunky at first. You can put them on, step into the snow, and you're on your way. Snowshoeing offers an outstanding workout if you choose to go far or to traverse hilly or steep terrain. Or you can take it easy on flatter ground.

Whatever your potential interest in either activity, the best thing about both cross-country skiing and snowshoeing is that they're healthy, quiet, self-propelled activities that make it especially easy to explore and enjoy the winter woods. There's no better way to stay in touch with snow-covered nature and experience the underrated beauty of our coldest season. Read elsewhere to learn more about these and other activities. Among available resources is my book *The Essential Guide to Cross-Country Skiing and Snowshoeing in the United States*, which recommends locations for these activities in thirty-eight states.

Other Activities

This chapter has surveyed some of the quieter, healthier, non-polluting, low-tech forms of outdoor recreation that are most conducive to communing with nature. Among other possibilities is horseback riding, which is especially popular in the western states but available throughout the country. Designated horse trails and other multiuse trails suitable for this purpose are found in many parks and wilderness areas.

Bicycling has long been a favored way of exploring country and park roads. During the past couple of decades the arrival of mountain biking has provided another two-wheeled option that has experienced phenomenal growth. On a mountain bike you can leave roadways to follow rougher and steeper park and forest trails, which make for a more thrilling and demanding ride. Because of their heavy impact on the trail environment as well as their potential conflict with foot travelers, mountain bikes are not allowed in some parks and designated wilderness areas, including the backcountry areas of most of our national parks.

More extreme and potentially dangerous sports like rock climbing and mountaineering have their passionate advocates as well. Much has been written about the sometimes harrowing and ecstatic experiences of those who attempt to "become one with the mountain" by climbing it, who put themselves and their bodies on the line in pursuit of the most difficult gravity-defying goals. However, the vast majority of us, even those of us who enjoy rigorous activities and exciting challenges, prefer somewhat safer and less dramatic means of communing with nature.

Other Ways of Being in Nature

Recreational activities tend to be exhilarating and quite habit-forming, but they comprise only a portion of the possibilities out in the natural world. Life also requires rest and the regathering of energies. Some people have the strength and motivation to spend almost all of their waking hours engaged in intense, single-minded activity. For the majority of us, however, this is a recipe for exhaustion or burnout. In or out of nature, it makes sense to plan a more balanced day.

For some of us, going into nature is a time to temporarily disconnect from goal-oriented activities and accomplishing anything—it's an opportunity to let go of striving and get off the treadmill of expectations. We find it refreshing to simply be in nature, either by ourselves or with one or more companions. We may not need to do very much at all except maybe meditate, contemplate, reflect, rest, or gently commune with the wild. These ways of being in nature are addressed throughout this book.

We may also want to enjoy the company of our friends, engage in intense or lighthearted discussions, question everything under the sun, tell stories and share past experiences, spend quiet evenings around a campfire, or stretch out on the ground for some stargazing. Or we may want to spend time in solitude, pondering, painting, sketching, writing, journaling, and whatever else. All of this, of course, takes place within the rich context of nature.

Among the more appealing aspects of being fully ensconced in the natural world, whether for a few hours or a few days, is that there's no phone to interrupt us (assuming we have the good sense to leave our cell phone at home), none of the other potential sources of disruption that can sometimes plague us, no newspapers to read or depressing world news to watch, no necessary chores or major responsibilities hanging over us, and nothing else to do beyond the most basic, most rewardingly ordinary requirements of life. This also makes it easier to experience the simple but profound joys of being alive. And nothing can keep us from living fully and completely in the present moment, which is one of the most valuable experiences we can have in nature.

Spending Time Safely in Nature

Is the natural world a dangerous place? No, contrary to what our movies and other media would sometimes have us believe—

as long as we know how to take care of ourselves there. Few places in the world are safer, in fact, for those of us who are experienced in outdoor living and travel. Serious accidents and other mishaps are surprisingly rare. You're much more likely to get hurt on a highway or in your own home than in the wild.

Like everywhere else, however, there are indeed some potential hazards and ways you could get in trouble, although a modicum of common sense will protect you from most of them. If you're a beginner, it's wise to read about safety issues and also learn from others by initially going with an organized group. Among the things you should know is how to use a map and compass to avoid getting lost, how to behave around wild animals when you encounter them, and how to minimize the risk of having an accident on foot, on skis, on your bike, or in watercraft.

The single most important skill that will serve you well in almost every situation is the ability to stay fully conscious, attentive, alert, and aware as you proceed through the natural world. The time to totally relax and space out is when you're sitting or lying down, not while you're moving. The ideal is to cultivate a kind of unstressful, cautious attentiveness that allows you to keep an eye out for problems and avoid mishaps while simultaneously enjoying yourself and the day's activity.

It's normal for novices to have fears regarding possible dangers, and these may have some basis in reality. If you feel anxious on a narrow, precipitous trail or a slippery hillside it's because there's a very real risk you could fall and hurt yourself, meaning it may be sensible to turn back. On the other hand, the common fears many people have regarding such creatures as bears and snakes are usually completely out of proportion to the actual danger. The chances of being attacked by a wild animal or bitten by a snake are truly miniscule. If you're careful, you could spend an entire lifetime in the natural world without even having a close call. Such fears often subside with experience in nature.

Seeing wildlife is usually a treat or a thrill, but we need to know how to act in their presence. Our paths can cross theirs at any time, often when we least expect it. Always stop in your tracks when you sight a wild animal. If it's behaving in a way that appears the least bit aggressive, slowly back off while continuing to face the animal. Do not shout. If it seems alarmed, speak softly and look off to one side rather than directly at it. Never, ever, go closer to a wild creature for any reason, including to take a photo, as your approach could appear threatening and might incite it to attack. Most often a large animal will retreat and be gone in moments, before you even have a chance to react or appreciate the encounter.

Clothing and Gear

What we wear may not be terribly important if we're only taking a short walk in nature, and we may not need to bring anything with us. Going some distance into the natural world is another story. It's essential that we wear and carry enough of the right clothing and suitable equipment. The weather could change and it could start to rain, the temperature could drop, or the wind could pick up, and without adequate clothing and rain gear we might find ourselves in real trouble.

Always bring more clothing than you think you'll need when spending time out in nature, in case it's cooler than expected. In cool or cold weather, avoid wearing cotton, especially next to your skin, as cotton provides no insulation when it gets wet from rain or sweat. Instead choose synthetics, silk, or wool. Use layering during the cooler seasons: dress in several thinner layers rather than wearing a heavy jacket or coat, so you can remove or add layers to keep your body the right temperature. Pay attention to how warm or cold you feel and adjust clothing frequently if necessary; don't wait until you get chilled or overheated.

Always bring rainwear as well unless you live in an area where rain is truly an impossibility. Remember that weather forecasts are often wrong, especially in mountain areas but elsewhere as well, so it's good to get in the habit of bringing rain protection regardless of the forecast. Sooner or later you'll get caught in a surprise storm and be extremely happy you have it along. Carry lightweight nylon rain gear—a poncho, rain parka, or rain jacket with pants—that is compact and will take up relatively little space in your pack.

Rounding out your outdoor wardrobe is your footwear, which is especially important for any physically active person. Suitable and comfortable walking shoes or hiking boots are essential items, particularly when you travel on rocky, rugged trails. Wearing the right footwear will reduce the chances of any injury if you trip or stumble, and they can help keep your feet dry. For walking enjoyment they should fit well and be truly comfortable.

Whenever you go out for an extended time or distance from a road, bring along a day pack to wear on your back. In it will go some of that extra clothing, as well as your rain gear and other essentials, including water, food, your first aid kit, other safety items, and your map and compass. It's extremely important to bring and drink adequate amounts of water, which should be carried in unbreakable plastic bottles or canteens. Proper hydration is mandatory for your well-being; remember to take in ample amounts of water throughout the day. Carry a minimum of a liter on an easy outing and up to a gallon on a long, hot-weather hike. Bring food as well if you'll be out for more than a couple of hours, especially if you'll be exercising vigorously, to meet your nutritional needs and keep your energy up. Adequate intake of food is critical as well for staying warm in cold weather.

Read outdoor recreation books for more detailed advice about what to bring on outings of different kinds. You'll often find checklists of appropriate items included. When you go, be diligent about carrying safety items and sufficient clothing, but otherwise keep what you bring simple and basic. Carry an interesting book to read if you like, but consider leaving escapist distractions at home. Don't even think about bringing a small radio or cassette player, which will keep you plugged into civilization and put up an auditory and psychological wall between you and nature. Aside from the necessities you bring, let your journey into the natural world be an intimate encounter between you and nature alone. Let this be an exciting and adventurous opportunity to reduce or erase the distance between you and the rest of the living world.

7

⬿

Venturing Deep
into the Wild

Wilderness areas and other totally wild or pristine places exert a strong pull on the hearts and imaginations of many of us. It's exciting to know there still are unspoiled realms where roads and public facilities are nonexistent, where nature reigns supreme, and where all forms of life fortunate enough to reside there are free to live out their destinies without human interference. And to know that these awe-inspiring spaces are open to our entry.

Nowhere is communing with nature more adventurous and thrillingly immediate than in the wilderness. Nowhere do we find such a fantastic variety of living things. Nowhere are there fewer obstacles or barriers to connecting. Nowhere is the modern world more absent. Nowhere is existence less adulterated or freedom more fully manifested. Nowhere is life more in balance.

Those of us who love wilderness may run the risk of romanticizing it at times. But we also need to acknowledge the darker side of wilderness and of life itself. There's the everyday violence of predator and prey, which we occasionally witness in wild areas, wherein some lives are sustained by the taking of other lives. In civilization this usually goes on behind closed doors, especially with "meat production," since we don't like to see or think about the killing involved. And we must remember that even those of us who are vegetarians must take the lives of plants to feed ourselves.

We could also consider the devastating effects of severe storms and extreme weather, which can be fatal to those caught out in it unprepared, as well as nature's often unforgiving response to those who become lost or injured, or find themselves in other trouble. Wilderness demands respect and offers no guarantees. Although we can keep risks to a minimum, we can't count on assistance if something goes wrong. If we choose to visit remote areas, we must take full responsibility for ourselves while there. One of the best teachings we receive from the wild is that hubris is harmful and humility helpful to our survival.

Wilderness and other natural areas have long been endangered by the ceaseless development that's eating up the countryside everywhere. Only because of the foresight of some of the more visionary leaders in the past century or so, along with the dedicated work of many environmental groups and activists, have so many wild areas been set aside for protection. Yet the remaining communities of untrammeled life need to be constantly defended against the efforts of exploiters who essentially seek to eliminate them in pursuit of profit.

Wilderness areas provide pleasure to the people who visit them, but they need to be protected for far more important reasons: they provide shelter and habitat for countless species, and they contribute vitally to the health of the planet as a whole and the well-being of all. Uncut forests absorb enormous amounts of the carbon dioxide we generate, for example, while at the same time produce the oxygen that we and other creatures need to breathe. Yet the assault on forests and wild areas has yet to be halted, including in such areas as our Pacific Northwest and the Amazon, where the logging of ancient rainforests continues to wipe out species, reduce biodiversity, and in the process put the long-term prospects for all of us at risk. And even protected areas can't be shielded from the widespread pollution, acid rain, and other harmful by-products of industry. Fortunately, wilderness now has more defenders than ever, and with sufficient public support we can hope that the tide will be turned toward greater preservation and the curbing of ecosystem abuses.

Visiting Wilderness

Wilderness isn't for everyone. Your average tourist or less-than-adventurous nature-lover isn't necessarily interested in exploring wild and roadless natural areas, nor should they consider doing so. Only those with the appropriate background or training—who know how to be totally self-sufficient and can take care of themselves in the widest possible range of conditions—should undertake solo wilderness travel.

If you happen to be someone who hears the siren call of the wild and you're fully prepared for it, some of the most exciting and memorable experiences of your life may await you. Few environments on the face of the planet are more interesting, inspiring, and often stunningly beautiful than those that are protected as wilderness areas, including the more remote portions of many of our national parks and national forests.

Should you be new to wilderness travel, go with a reputable group or experienced friends the first few times. Consider taking a wilderness survival course as well, and read a book or two on the subject. If you haven't spent much time in nature, first devote a number of days to visiting and exploring smaller, tamer parks and sanctuaries. Don't test fate by going alone or with unseasoned companions. Although wilderness excursions tend to be reasonably safe when you know what you're doing, beginners may make some potentially life-threatening blunders.

Wilderness Activities and Their Effects

Most but not all people who venture into wilderness areas follow established trails or waterways. Recreational activities like hiking or canoeing are usually built into a wilderness trip, especially when we're traveling more than a short distance into the wild. Many of the outdoor activities discussed in the previous chapter are pertinent to wilderness trips, and camping is often part of the equation because of the remoteness of many tracts. While it's possible to take day trips into large parks and wilderness areas, if you have to turn back within a few hours you'll probably only be able to visit the most accessible places that are convenient to entry points; these also tend to be the most heavily visited areas. If you're able to stay for several days or more, however, you can go much deeper into the backcountry. For a detailed treatment of wilderness camping and where it's legal to camp in the wild throughout the country, see my book *The*

Essential Guide to Wilderness Camping and Backpacking in the United States.

When you hike into the wilderness with a full-size backpack, carrying everything you need to camp for one or more nights, the activity is usually called backpacking—one of the most popular recreational ways of enjoying wilderness areas. It's equally possible to explore the wild in a canoe, kayak, or raft where there are suitable waterways; or on horseback; or on cross-country skis or snowshoes; or even on a mountain bike in the limited number of locations where it's permitted in wilderness areas.

While the form of recreational travel we choose will often be the primary focus of an extended trip, we can also stay put in one place as long as we want. For some of us the ideal trip offers major expanses of free time for communing with the wild. During these leisurely and luxurious hours or days we can devote ourselves to connecting with nature to whatever extent we wish, and explore many of the options for enhancing our relationship with the wild that are discussed in this book.

Those of us who plan to cover some distance within a wilderness area should avoid committing to an overly ambitious itinerary or schedule, especially if we're in other than excellent shape. And we should remember to allow for inclement weather, along with the possibility of pulled muscles or other problems that could lead to delays. Since most of us don't want a wilderness adventure to become an endurance contest, a sensible plan usually includes rest days and enough spare time to meet other needs. For maximum enjoyment, allow for the unexpected, for spontaneity and serendipity, and for the option of amending plans should needs or circumstances dictate.

On a longer trip our bodies have more time to adjust to the activity. Eventually the flow of physical movement may come to feel utterly natural, right, and almost effortless. We'll sometimes find ourselves in a serene or even blissful state, which may include feeling at one with the trail or waterway, our greater surroundings, and sometimes with the world at large. These experiences tend to be altogether too rare and elusive in everyday life. Getting into that endorphin-enriched flow may put us at risk of becoming addicted to the activity, which has the benefit of greatly increasing the odds that we'll return to nature and the wilderness at our earliest convenience. Little harm and much good can come from becoming hooked on wilderness activities, as long as we don't go so overboard that the rest of our life suffers; they'll often help instill in us a lasting appreciation of the wild.

Experiencing Wilderness

What happens to us when we spend days on end away from the din of civilization? When wild nature has an opportunity to really go to work on our minds and bodies? As we might reasonably expect, it's impossible to return from an extended wilderness trip in a frame of mind that resembles the one we arrived with. We're bound to feel different, sometimes remarkably so, and even to look different. Unless things have somehow gone awry, we usually reemerge feeling markedly better than before.

The therapeutic effects bear some similarities to those we may experience from spending time in our local park, but in the wilderness these effects are much more intensified and concentrated. When we stay in nature both day and night, we're continuously exposed to positive energies and influences that are prone to uplift or heal us. The only downside is the trouble we may have tearing ourselves away to return home and the pain we may feel in readjusting to the less natural and less desirable aspects of everyday life; this can, however, help push us to change how we live.

On an extended wilderness trip our sense of time is totally transformed. Here it's transparent how artificial and in some respects unhealthy it is for us to experience each day largely in terms of the hours, minutes, and seconds we divide it into. Aside from the natural monthly lunar cycle and daily solar cycle, our measures of time are invented. The arbitrary fracturing of time into small segments doesn't fit life well, especially in the wild. We're better off packing the watch away, in fact, and allowing the unfolding of each wilderness day to proceed without counting hours. The most important reason to consult a timepiece is when we're involved in some activity during the day and need to pace ourselves—to avoid being caught out in the dark away from our camp or the road leading home. On a clear day we can use the sun to tell the approximate time, but in foggy or inclement weather it's easy to lose track.

In the wilderness we may get a clearer sense of how being prisoners of clock time pressures and stresses us in everyday life. How many of us go through our workdays constantly running late, always trying to catch up with where we're supposed to be in our overbooked schedules and rarely finding the time to relax? Measured time can be a tyrant, and too many of us freely turn our power over to the clock. One of the reasons why the natural world tends to be such a relaxing place is that clock time matters so little in this realm. There's no better place than the wilderness to lose our time-obsession; putting our watches away will help us break the habit of consulting them so often. The wilderness is also a good setting for practicing letting go of any tendencies we have to engage in compulsive schedule-keeping.

It can be delightful to forget what day of the week it is as well, which sometimes occurs on a trip of several days or more. After all, there's no newspaper, news report, or calendar to keep reminding us of the date. To some of us, experiencing such freedom from schedules feels like true luxury. Another concept that loses much of its meaning in the wild is money. There's no need whatsoever for it here, absolutely nothing to spend it on, and no way to purchase anything we might have forgotten to bring. So money's artificial and symbolic nature becomes especially apparent.

Some Rewarding Absences

Another element of an extended wilderness trip is the quiet we're immersed in. It's rarely a true silence since nature is home to a host of intermittently vocal creatures and insects, and we're often serenaded as well by the sounds of wind and water. The one time it's sometimes possible to experience a profound stillness is in winter, especially when the landscape is blanketed with snow. And although crickets, croaking frogs, and howling coyotes may take some getting used to, almost all of the sounds we hear are natural, reasonably easy on the ears, and interesting.

The total absence of nerve-jarring noise from traffic, machinery, and other elements of civilization feels like a special blessing, and we start to get an inkling of how much our nervous and sensory systems may suffer from exposure to the ceaseless racket of everyday life. Only the occasional airplane overhead reminds us of how common such sounds are at home and how rare it is to be even temporarily free of them.

Missing here as well are most of the technologies we surround ourselves with in daily life and have come to be so dependent on, ranging from basic tools of civilization to the latest high-tech gadgetry—including hot running water, flushing toilets, heaters, furnaces, air conditioners, electric stoves, refrigerators, washing machines, motorized vehicles, telephones, radios, TVs, CD players, computers, and so on. Portable versions of some of these items could indeed be carried into the natural world, especially if we're staying at a campground where electrical hookups are available. But this would almost completely defeat our purposes in visiting nature and the wild. What high-tech and even low-tech addicts often don't realize is how greatly these technologies influence our lives and help separate us from nature, the earth, and even our own souls.

Some wilderness campers are initially surprised at how satisfying it can be to live for a time with a minimum of technology. Not only doesn't it feel like deprivation, but it's often one of the most refreshing and gratifying aspects of wilderness travel. We do use the technologies furnished by the basic equipment and clothing we bring along, but this is a far cry from being plugged into the grid. This isn't to say that most of us want to resign our membership in the modern world and retire to a cave. But simplifying our existence by eliminating some of the technological clutter can be part of a path to self-fulfillment, and it can be a way to erase some of the hurdles we've erected between ourselves and the community of nature.

A wilderness excursion can be the perfect occasion for practicing the art of simplifying, starting by bringing a minimum of items beyond the necessities of food, clothing, and other essential gear. This is a challenge for some beginners, who may be tempted to bring along almost everything under the sun "in case it's needed." In this culture that celebrates material abundance and conspicuous consumption, it's easy to fear the consequences of being without what we think we need or want. Yet a wonderful sense of freedom comes from not being weighed down by many possessions and their maintenance.

Another welcome absence we find in the wilderness is people, except in some wilderness areas in our most famous and overcrowded national parks. The typical human population density in the wild is extremely low, partly because of the sometimes demanding requirements of wilderness travel and the remoteness of many areas. If we avoid well-known routes or get off the beaten path, we're almost assured of finding solitude.

Those of us who appreciate the infrequency of meeting others in the wilderness aren't necessarily antisocial and may, in fact, love sharing experiences in nature with others. But more than a few of us already encounter a plethora of people in our work or social lives back home. It's not only pleasant and relaxing to take a vacation from humanity, but it's also delightful to be so outnumbered by other species and to be able to devote most of our attention to the rest of the living world for a change.

One final joy to note is the gratifying lack of fences and manmade boundaries in large wilderness areas. This is virtually the only place we can go in the world where we're not constantly reminded of political or property lines—where the landscape hasn't been artificially carved up by people into fenced tracts.

Here nature appears to have near-absolute rights, including to be left alone, and the ecosystem is allowed to flourish totally unencumbered and unrestrained. Here nature isn't subject to humanity's whims, although the protection of wilderness areas could be withdrawn if our political leaders should ever marshal enough support to eliminate it. And here we, too, can roam freely far and wide without concern for boundaries, barriers, territorial limits, or other restrictions.

Wilderness Adventures

While one of our major reasons for spending time in a wilderness area will often be to commune with nature, as well as to relax and perhaps "escape from everyday life," some of us also respond to the call of adventure. A backpacking or canoeing trip puts us in a direct, primal relationship with the elements of the wild—with the wind and water, the soil and sand, the sun and stars. We're touched and sometimes tested by what we meet. A true adventure engages us physically, sensually, and soulfully in a way that more sedentary activities can never begin to do.

We certainly don't have to risk our necks to get the most out of a wilderness outing. For some of us the perfect weekend outing will consist of quiet nature study or a wilderness meditation retreat. But for others among us risk-taking will be more a part of the picture. Even though few of us are drawn to more dangerous activities like mountaineering, many of us are willing to take calculated risks, both in the wilderness and at home, in order to grow, experience more of life's possibilities, gain a sense of accomplishment, and perhaps test ourselves. Whatever we choose to do, we should observe sensible limits and know when to turn back from potential danger, which we can learn by going out with seasoned outdoorspeople.

Wilderness Awakenings

The wilderness can be a life-changing place for us if we spend enough time there and open ourselves to its splendor and mystery. Few environments are more potentially transformative for us, since in the wild we're so removed from ordinary life and the hyperactivity of civilization's ceaseless input and so surrounded by nature's life-enhancing effects. And while a wilderness trip can be almost anything we want it to be, it will often affect and alter us in ways we never could have imagined.

In religious traditions the wilderness has always been a place to go for spiritual renewal. The awakenings of famous religious leaders have largely taken place in wilderness areas, and people worldwide continue to make pilgrimages to mountains, deserts, and other wild areas in search of spiritual guidance, especially in times of crisis. Native peoples in our own country sent children who were coming of age into the wild alone to pursue vision quests and receive direction from their creator.

Whether or not we're on a particular spiritual path, there's no better setting on earth than the wilderness for going deep within, for exploring our innermost being, and for searching for answers to the most challenging questions life can pose. What we'll discover or conclude can't possibly be foretold. And there's no better place in the world than the wild for reaching out to nature and allowing her truths to inform and potentially illuminate us.

Whatever our reasons for wanting to visit the wilderness (which may include physical, psychological, emotional, or spiritual purposes) and however we choose to spend our time, we're wise to keep our expectations wide open. We need to leave room for the possibility of wonder, astonishment, or joy overtaking us; for changes in our perspectives and perceptions regarding self, nature, wilderness, and the world at large; and for new beginnings, awarenesses, and awakenings.

8

⚜

COMING FULLY TO
OUR SENSES

WE'RE SENSORY BEINGS—like most other creatures we share the planet with. It's through our senses that the world comes to life for us. These extraordinary capacities actually guide and shape every moment of our day, every aspect of our existence. They make it possible for us to interact in countless ways with others and the rest of the universe. Every experience we have is mediated by them. Just try for a moment to imagine living without them.

As we do with so many other things in life, we tend to take our senses for granted until we slowly or suddenly lose one of them. We rarely appreciate their potential richness and reach, or realize what miraculous abilities they really are. This seems to be another example of our blindness to some of the more amazing aspects of the human body and nature, which is a characteristic apparently associated with our adoption of "civilized" ways.

Our senses have suffered most from our withdrawal from the natural world, which has only been fully accomplished in the modern era. By settling in noisy cities and synthetic suburbs—and especially by moving our activities indoors—we've deprived our senses of the range of conditions and stimuli they require for optimal functioning. We've also reduced their acuity by overloading them with too much negative input.

We now make demands of our sense organs that they were never designed to handle. It shouldn't be surprising that we have deteriorating eyesight and need glasses, for example, considering all the close-up work and reading we do indoors, where we're unable to shift our focus to more distant objects on the horizon, and where the lighting is unnatural and often inadequate. Hearing losses can only be expected among the many of us who are exposed to high-decibel noise or music on a frequent basis. We can't blame our sense of smell for retreating in the presence of noxious fumes and other unpleasant odors, including those of air pollution, that many of us routinely inhale. Our taste buds may not be similarly under assault, but they're not exactly enlivened by the unstimulating supermarket fare and fast foods we often subject them to. Even touch has trouble holding its own in the modern world: we're not taught or encouraged to make physical contact with others or the earth, and many of us have no idea how much information and feeling we're missing out on.

Numbness is now almost the norm in our culture, at least for an alarming number of people. Some of us seem to be experiencing a sort of sensory shutdown: there's too much coming at us from the world to take in, and more than a little of it is unpleasant, so our bodies and minds deal with the overload by restricting the input; thus our overstimulated senses become numb. Increasingly intense stimuli are often required to elicit any reaction at all from us.

So what's to be done for our weary, embattled senses? The answer is no secret, and it should be no mystery to readers of this book: what our senses need most is nature. The best therapy for numbed or stressed senses is thorough immersion in the natural world, where they've always been most at home. Paradoxically, nature is also the appropriate place to take *understim*ulated senses (for the ever-shrinking minority who are isolated from the clamor of modern life), since most natural landscapes are overflowing with interesting stimuli. If our senses are nature-deprived, they'll initially be overwhelmed upon entering the wild, but it's also where they will experience the most complete healing.

Sight

To renew your vision, feast your tired eyes on nature. Civilization's linear world offers relatively little to nourish or enhance our sight and plenty of stressful effects to tire it out. For example, while there's no denying that some of our towns and villages are extremely attractive, uninspiring landscapes and eyesores unfortunately abound throughout the land. Compare the number of visual treats you encounter in the nearest developed area with those you find on even the shortest trip into nature.

Almost everything in the natural world is potentially interesting to the eyes, and most elements are restful to them as well. We do need to protect these precious visual receptors from direct sunlight, dust, and other intrusions, but there's no place on earth they're more suited to than nature. Our eyes usually begin roaming freely and widely as soon as we enter the wild, where they're liberated from the restricted regimen we subject them to. Far more shapes, forms, and shadings of light and color are found here than anywhere in the man-made world.

Although relationships and repetitive patterns are rampant in nature, nothing here is as uniformly predictable in the visual sphere as it is back at home, where most of the surfaces we walk on are flat, most rooms and buildings are box-shaped, and the objects of everyday life are organized in systematic ways. Few surprises meet our eyes on an average day at home.

Nature is indeed much "messier," but we nevertheless find our eyes and bodies drawn almost magnetically to the dense displays of vegetation, the seeming chaos of teeming life, and the disorderly but gorgeous "refuse" of spruce needles, pine cones, and small plants that may carpet the forest floor. The fatigue our eyes feel after a long day in nature is usually an extremely pleasant tiredness, unlike the tense, headachy eyestrain from too many hours of office work.

When viewed at a distance with totally untrained eyes, nature may be something of a green and brown blur at first, with some other colors perhaps mixed in. But before long, an amazing variety of flora, fauna, and other forms come into increasingly sharp focus for us. In time we can learn to distinguish and identify dozens if not hundreds of individual species, including creatures that initially avoid our detection by their protective coloration or by remaining still while we pass.

Let your eyes lead you forward into nature and take you into the hidden places they seem to want to explore. At the same time, they should serve as sentries on the lookout for possible hazards. When stopping for a break, relax and allow your sight to sink into the rippling waters of a lake, river, or brook, carrying your mind along to rest in the peaceful depths. Or, gaze softly at leaves and grasses as they nod back and forth in a breeze or are tossed in the wind, and let your thoughts drift back and forth with them. You may find yourself gaining access to some unexplored chambers of your imagination. Let your eyes be embraced by the natural landscape as it fills and floods them.

Eyes touched and taught by nature will never see the rest of the world in quite the same way again. They'll smart if we bring them back to the everyday world too abruptly, but in time they may bring us clearer and sharper perceptions of almost everything we encounter. And sight that's been mentored by nature can help us achieve insight.

Hearing

Almost everyone responds positively to nature's sounds. Their beneficial effects are many, including the way they amplify our ability to detect distant sounds and distinguish between them. Some natural sounds can be scary to the uninitiated, especially at night—for instance, the shrieks of certain larger birds, the howls of wolves or coyotes, and other ominous-sounding calls or vocalizations that we can't identify. But most sounds of nature are absolute music to our ears, with an effect that tends to be reliably soothing or otherwise extremely pleasant.

Few of us fail to appreciate (and many of us truly love) the lilting songs of birds, which bring the open fields and forests exuberantly to life during the warmer months. Equally irresistible are the delicious and mesmerizing sounds of water, which seductively call out to us from lakeshores with their lapping waves and from rushing streams and waterfalls. Also appealing are the restful, comforting whispers and whistles of breezes and winds as they blow through leaves, grasses, and other vegetation (except during storms, when they become much louder and more appropriately disturbing, encouraging us to retreat).

Notice the range of sounds around you whenever you're in nature, attempt to identify their sources, and enjoy their restful serenade. Some of them could have a healing effect on your hearing, especially if it has suffered from abuse or overload during your lifetime. One of the many pleasures of visiting wild places is the refreshing and delightful sound environment. Not only is the overall volume much lower here, but there are times of near-total silence, particularly in late fall and winter. We should try to get out of earshot of roads since traffic noise can drown out the more subtle sounds and distract us from our enjoyment. We can't prevent an occasional airplane from passing overhead, but by removing ourselves from most man-made sounds, we can listen to nature's symphony in relative peace.

Natural sounds help induce a meditative state, especially when we're relaxing or not otherwise distracted, and this is one of the many positive effects we experience in the natural environment. The sounds and silence of nature are conducive to a lowering of tension in the human body. If you have a meditation practice, or otherwise choose to meditate in nature, you can use these sounds to enrich the process. Instead of focusing on your breathing, try attending to the repetitive sounds of birdcalls, chirping crickets, or lapping waves.

When we spend time in a "soup" of natural sounds, we feel our entire body becoming infused with the reverberations. And as can happen through our other senses, bathing in natural sound helps us internalize nature so that she becomes more a part of us and lodges deep inside us. Later on, back in the din of everyday life, these sounds may continue to echo within us.

Smell

A walk in nature during the warmer seasons exposes us to an endless array of tantalizing scents, some of which we'll usually be unfamiliar with. Thousands of fragrances and other more pungent smells can be experienced in the course of exploring the natural world. Compare this abundance with our often sterile or "air-freshened" indoor environments; only the kitchen is likely to offer a passable collection of appealing and reasonably natural aromas.

Even before civilization, the human sense of smell appears to have been inferior to that of many other animals, but it has been drastically diminished in the modern era. Our olfactory systems have especially suffered from centuries of foul odors from heavy industry and polluted air, which continue to damage the cells of our nasal passages and throats to this very day. Some of us have had our sense of smell so desensitized that it requires a strong odor for us to take any notice at all.

As with our other senses, the best antidote by far is nature, including spending time in our gardens or with flowering plants in our homes and workplaces. Waking up our sense of smell can be a slow process, but the more time we spend in nature and the more we stop to smell the flora, the more our olfactory nerves are likely to be restored. Inhale deeply through your nose and observe the sensations and feelings that follow.

Try following your nose into nature by taking a scent-oriented stroll. Bring each aroma or smell into your awareness, locate its source if you can, and allow it to enter your breathing passages and body. Does the scent have an apparent function, such as to attract birds or insects for pollination? Most of us have favorite fragrances that we look forward to finding. Some scents come to represent a locale or season for us.

Springtime in nature is a gift for our sense of smell, given the explosion of flowers and fresh new growth that fills the air with so many aromas of life that it's hard to process them all. Another excellent time to be out is during or after rain, when the earth opens up and releases delectable scents into the air. Even natural odors that are commonly considered offensive, such as those of animal droppings or skunk spray, have a rich, natural earthiness. We wouldn't want to use them as perfumes, but they have infinitely more appeal than civilization's synthetic smells.

Taste

Until relatively recently all of our food came from nature, and even now our diet still largely consists of flora-and-fauna-based products, but they're often in highly processed and altered states. Sadly, the taste of most modern food falls far short of practically anything on nature's menu. We can all tell the difference, for instance, between fresh, delicious garden vegetables and their bland, uninspiring supermarket equivalents.

Growing some of our own food is one solution. It's a good way to stimulate our taste buds, improve our nutrition, and maybe at the same time strengthen our connection with nature. We can also find reasonably healthy and tasty fare in natural food stores. Out in nature herself our options are regrettably somewhat limited now, given the understandable restrictions on harvesting vegetation in many public parks, and given the fact that most of us no longer have the knowledge to identify wild edibles. Since there's a risk of poisoning ourselves, we need to be serious students of wild plants or mushrooms in order to supplement our diet with them in a substantial way. Berries and other natural fruits do make delightful snacks when they're in season, however, and licensed fishing or hunting are permitted in many areas.

The fresher and more natural the foods you can find for your diet, the healthier, sharper, and more satisfied your taste buds are probably going to be. You may personally find certain popular processed foods irresistible, and the majority of us are addicted to them, but if you pay attention you'll notice that these foods don't accentuate your sensory awareness but rather tend to blunt it. Most important, nature's fare nourishes our bodies, minds, and souls much better than the adulterated, artificial, and often empty foods endlessly marketed to us.

Touch

We benefit from actually touching the earth and other elements of the natural world as often as possible. As physical beings, we learn best and connect most fully by making personal contact with the world. If a tree looks interesting to you, or you've been using it as a backrest, spend a bit of time exploring the bark and trunk with your hands. Afterward you'll have a vivid memory of it, and the tree may mean more to you.

Approach every form of vegetation with a bit of caution, however, before you touch it. Be careful to stay clear of such plants as poison ivy, poison oak, poison sumac, and stinging nettles. If you're not already familiar with them, get a field guide that shows you which ones to avoid and what they look like. Also beware of species that are protected by sharp thorns or needles, and when you pass bushes or trees, watch for sharp branches that you could inadvertently walk into and poke yourself with. And when getting close to vegetation be sure you're not disturbing any concealed wildlife. Wild animals should never be touched, of course; never assume it's safe to approach and pet or otherwise touch a small, seemingly unassuming creature, which could bite or claw you in an instant if it feels threatened. Always observe wildlife from a distance.

The tactile pleasures of exploring the rest of nature with our hands and body are many. Who can resist stroking moss, soft leaves, smooth rocks, or seashells? Who isn't tempted to stretch out in a meadow, walk barefoot in the sand, or wade into a bubbling stream on a summer day? Not only does having physical contact with nature enable us to get to know the earth better and learn more about each element and being, but it also awakens our body, which probably sits dormant at a desk or curled up on a couch much of the time. When we put the sensory receptors in our skin in touch with nature's sensuous surfaces, they shout their approval.

Other Senses

It's possible to hypothesize the existence of other senses—since our traditional five senses can't account for all of the information we receive from the world. Much that we sense about other people, for example, seems to be on an energetic or intuitive level. Many of the things we learn about nature and other beings come not only from the direct reception of "raw sense data" but from the feelings we have while in their presence and within their energy fields. Intuitions that we can't verify via our other senses may operate in this realm. But our understanding of such energies and their effects on us remains extremely limited and primitive.

Whether we could indeed be said to have other senses, or whether this is a matter of picking up on more subtle cues, these abilities should be more easily developed and refined in nature—considering how much less "static" and other disruptive influences we find there, which may otherwise interfere with our ability to receive or detect less obvious information. Given the absence of civilization's visual and auditory distractions, as well as the possibly interfering effects of the electromagnetic radiation that now swamps our developed environments, there's no doubt that in the natural world it's easier to tune in to what's going on.

9

Harmonizing
with Nature

WHEN WE LIVED entirely as a part of nature, the rhythms of our lives and bodies were synchronized with those of the earth, as remains the case for all living things that still reside in the wild. It was impossible to exist otherwise—until we invented electricity and other technologies that allowed us to ignore natural cycles and create a new world for ourselves.

What our forebears had no way of knowing is that removing ourselves from natural processes would come at a considerable cost. Although human beings are well-known for their ability to adapt to a wide range of conditions, our well-being suffers when our ways diverge too widely from nature's. Going against the natural grain stresses and unbalances us. Our minds and bodies don't function as well when we're out of sync with nature.

The daily cycle of light and dark is one of several cycles that we've tried to ignore in modern times. Although few of us would want to do without the convenience of indoor lighting, especially during the darker winter months, consider how many of us suffer from chronic sleep deficits because we now try to pack so much into our days and nights; or the sleep problems among those who work rotating or night shifts; or the fact that by rarely leaving our lit-up world we miss witnessing the spectacular night sky.

Turning in early and rising with the sun, as earth-based peoples do, seems to be the most natural way for human beings, and it's probably the healthiest. This is the pattern our bodies still appear to prefer, although some night owls may disagree. Most of us feel better, are more alert during our waking hours, and sleep best when we follow such a schedule. Doing so in our culture isn't exactly easy, however, given how many social and other activities we regularly reserve for the evening hours.

By developing climate-controlled environments, we've also been able to step almost completely out of the cycle of seasons. Central heating in winter and air-conditioning in summer serve to increase our level of comfort and offer protection from temperature extremes, but they don't permit our bodies to acclimate as they should. One result of spending most of our hours indoors within a narrow range of temperatures is that we become chilled or overheated outdoors much more quickly than we would otherwise. And at the same time, we've come to fear cold and inclement weather unnecessarily, whereas with the right clothing and attitude we can adapt more easily to such conditions.

Another cycle we've come to ignore is that of the moon, which appears to have effects on our bodies and behavior that we're only now beginning to acknowledge and understand. These influences were long recognized and allowed for by traditional societies but until recently were dismissed as superstition in our own. Aside from the observed effects on womens' menstrual cycles, evidence from research reveals differences in human creativity, violence, and other behaviors at different times of the lunar cycle, with a peak of activity typically coinciding with the full moon. It's interesting to see how ancient teachings are increasingly being validated by modern science—additional evidence for the wisdom of readopting ways of living that are more in sync with natural cycles.

Slowing Down

Activity ebbs and flows in nature. And there's a lot of downtime in the natural world: most creatures devote many hours to sleeping or resting, and larger mammals are sometimes inactive for long periods, especially during the colder months. To the casual observer, not a lot seems to be happening in the wild most of the time, which is only partly because many creatures conceal themselves and remain dormant during the day. Few animals, in fact, are as busy as some members of our own species, who rush around in a futile attempt to accomplish more than is humanly possible in a lifetime.

Nature's pace is much slower; there are bursts of intense activity, but these are interspersed with large intervals of rest. We would benefit enormously if we could adjust our own routines accordingly and allow ample time for regathering our energies and recharging our batteries. This is likely to increase our overall enjoyment of life. It's difficult to greet the dawn with joy and savor the beautiful moments if we're perpetually immersed in a fog of fatigue or exhaustion. Collectively we appear to be addicted to activity, and our culture's values support working to excess for material gain, so we're rarely willing to acknowledge our need for rest and reflection. No wonder so many of us find ourselves feeling drained and spent.

The slowest time of year in nature is winter, which we've learned to race through just like any other season—overworking ourselves, getting run down, and sometimes becoming sick in the process. A much healthier and more natural alternative would be to reduce our activity, turn inward for a time, perhaps engage in some self-examination, and get internally ready for the activities and challenges of the coming season.

How, then, do we extricate ourselves from this treadmill of endless activity, this self-defeating cycle that rarely lets us catch up on rest and sets us up for burnout? One answer is to spend more of our hours in the natural world, where we may be more easily coaxed out of our unhealthful habits. Here we can let ourselves be influenced and guided by nature's examples, which will help lead us toward a more balanced way of life.

Living More Naturally

Harmonizing with nature means honoring and respecting natural ways, including through our actions. This orientation can easily be self-sustaining since the most natural way of doing something tends to be the most satisfying. It's reassuring to know that this approach is usually the most ecologically sound one as well. Harmonizing also invites us to embrace the more natural rhythms, needs, and inclinations we find within ourselves.

We're all aware that such a perspective is far from the dominant one in our culture. We constantly hear from promoters of progress, merchants of dreams, and techno-enthusiasts who would have us believe that we can live any way we want, without regard for our natural underpinnings, and that we can vastly improve upon what nature has given us. Some of us have become convinced that the only real boundaries in life are the limits of our imaginations. While there may be a kernel of truth there, it's a mistake to assume that we can ever totally abandon our natural inclinations or our identities as earth-based beings. Too many of our previous attempts to ignore or violate the natural order have already had disastrous consequences: witness the unconscionable ways we've disfigured the face of the earth and undermined the life-support systems of so many of our planet's residents.

We learn from nature and ecology that healthy life systems are characterized by considerable amounts of stability, order, and balance. So although we're all entitled and invited to envision new and better ways of living for ourselves, and our man-made world certainly needs major improvements, we risk untoward consequences if we fail to include nature in our equations or to integrate natural ways into our plans and agendas. We're usually wise to go slowly and to try to maintain an equilibrium within our lives and the activities we pursue rather than rushing or lurching forward in our zeal to make changes. With nature's guidance we can keep our bearings.

Harmonizing with nature is easier when our lives are less hectic, less complicated, less materially oriented, and less plugged into the high-tech electronic world. This doesn't mean we have to part with our possessions, give up our favorite TV shows, or cease surfing the Internet, but our culture is notorious for coming up with a nearly infinite number of options for keeping us preoccupied. Choosing to spend most of our time in these ways precludes the possibility of communing with nature.

The simpler and more natural our way of life, the more likely it is that nature will find a prominent and permanent place there. Many of us need to exercise some discipline to weed out the unnecessary, unfulfilling, and time-wasting activities and technologies, and make room for the more important things, nature among them. While it isn't always easy to resist the advertising industry's attractive and manipulative attempts to increase our wants, to live a good life it's sometimes necessary to draw the line. How far you want to go with simplifying, and whether you want to go this route at all, is up to you.

Accepting and Respecting the Natural

Some of us have developed the unfortunate habit of finding fault with almost everything in the world, including nature and our own selves. We're rarely satisfied with the way things are or what we have. And while it makes sense to alter any aspects of our lives we don't like, our culture goes overboard in attempting to remake and improve upon "the natural order," including the natural elements, qualities, and processes we come in contact with or that comprise our very beings.

Many of us, for example, spend our entire lives feeling dissatisfied with some aspect or other of our physical appearance.

This has been greatly encouraged by the advertising industry, which would have us see ourselves as so lacking that we become regular consumers of products and services that promise self-improvement. Aside from cosmetics and other beauty aids, think of the millions of people who submit to plastic surgery or undergo grueling and often excessive body training in order to meet some imagined ideal. Is this a wise use of time, energy, and money? Why are we unable to love and accept ourselves as we are?

A more controversial example might be the extraordinary expense and effort that are sometimes invested in keeping dying people alive. All life must come to an end, and our bodies are made to wear out after a number of decades, whether we like it or not. We often forget that if scientists were ever to find a "cure for dying" or a way to greatly extend the human life span, the results would be absolutely catastrophic for the earth, which would be totally overrun with our species. Losing loved ones will always be painful, and it's indeed difficult for many of us to let go of our own lives when our time is up, but we also need to acknowledge and accept the realities that come with being born into this world. Our denial of death and resistance to the process ultimately cause a great deal of unnecessary suffering, not to mention expense.

Turning to the everyday realm of obtaining the food we eat, it's a given that certain foods can only grow in certain seasons. Yet we expend enormous energy and expense, including for costly fuel and transport that generate considerable amounts of air and water pollution in the process, to truck or ship food great distances so we can obtain anything we like at any time of year. If we were aware that this isn't good for the earth, would we be willing to consider giving up our attachment to having everything when, where, and how we want it? Living more naturally would prescribe that we try to purchase local foods in season whenever possible, and to get them directly from small farmers rather than give our dollars to the factory-food megacorporations.

At the same time, we should be careful to avoid turning a concern about living naturally into an obsession. It doesn't help for us to be overly rigid about avoiding the nonnatural, to get stressed out, or to beat up on ourselves when we fall short of the ideal. But it's always worth choosing the more natural alternative when we can, and it's worth remembering what we stand to benefit by adopting more natural lifestyles. We must never forget how much the earth loses from civilization's nonnatural ways of living—including the enormous waste and toxic pollution that's created in manufacturing the products we don't really need, the exhaust that spews from the cars we often drive unnecessarily, and the damage our consumption patterns ultimately wreak on the natural landscape. Among the results are such travesties as strip-mined mountains and clear-cut ancient forests. If we could reduce our wants and make do with less, nature would benefit, as would the quality of our everyday lives, as would our souls. In acting accordingly we would need less income to meet our needs, meaning we might have more free time for the things that matter most to us.

Increasing Inner Harmony

The degree of inner harmony or disharmony we experience is strongly influenced by the environments we occupy and how natural our way of life is. Those of us who spend ample time in natural surroundings usually find ourselves feeling more relaxed, centered, balanced, and in tune with our inner selves while we're there. When too many of our waking hours are lived in less-than-healthy, stressful, and nature-deficient realms, our moods are often negative, problems seem to be intensified or exacerbated, and we tend to feel disconnected from our truest selves.

Thus the more natural we can make our everyday existence, the more harmonious our inner world will probably become. Any difficulties we face will frequently be ameliorated by a natural physical environment and lifestyle, which are more conducive to maintaining a calm, clear, collected, and relaxed state of mind. When we do become upset or out of balance, which happens every now and then to most of us, we'll recover our equilibrium more quickly. So whether or not we avail ourselves of a meditation practice, achieving a sense of equanimity and inner peacefulness is within our reach if we choose to take nature as our guide.

Locating Our Place in the Ecological Web

The study of ecology can teach us much about life, including the many interrelationships among different species, which can help us learn to harmonize with nature. Until ecology came along, we didn't understand the importance of many species, the roles they play in the ecosystem, and how all the different participants are related. One of the most basic and important messages of ecology is that "we're all connected." Removing or controlling one species can have unexpected effects on others, which is why our attempts to manipulate nature so often backfire.

Science still remains ignorant about many natural processes and relationships, and this is one reason why we have an obligation to use extreme restraint in our attempts to alter the natural world. Should we trust the proponents of genetic engineering, for example, and believe their promises of safety when there are so many unknowns and no long-term studies? Claims regarding the safety and supposedly superior benefits of new products and technologies have proven false too many times in the past. Aside from urging our leaders to take actions to safeguard the public and the environment at large, we can help by making sure our own actions are consistently respectful of other species and the earth.

Consider the question of where you fit into the ecological web. Do you have a sense of your natural connections with other species? When you see different plants and animals, can you identify some of the ecologically defined relationships you may share with them? Can you see how these might be influenced by where and how you live, your eating habits, and your other patterns of consumption? Learning more about the web of life and where you and your species belong in it can give you additional ideas and insights about how to live more naturally and harmoniously.

Getting into the Flow of Life

The majority of us have experienced the wonderful feeling of flow, when whatever we're doing becomes incredibly easy or effortless, and things seem to move along exactly the way they should. This occurs most often with an activity we love and that comes as second nature to us. Common examples that many of us have enjoyed include dancing, singing, other creative activities, lovemaking, running, sports, and outdoor recreation.

Among the ultimate rewards of harmonizing with nature is how it gets us in sync with the natural flow of life both within us and outside of us. The requirement here is that we open ourselves fully to nature's ways and allow them free expression through us. Getting into the flow of life won't eliminate all of the problems or struggles we must contend with, but it can easily reduce some of the daily wear and tear on our psyches, and at the same time it can greatly intensify our joy of living. In the end, what more could we ask for than a reliable source of contentment with the possibility of some ecstatic intervals? We should keep such things in mind when we consider committing to more natural ways, or when we allow nature full entry into the innermost recesses of our being.

10

❦

CONNECTING WITH
THE LAND

WE NEED TO DEVELOP a relationship with the land that lies beneath our feet—to befriend the particular parcels of earth we live on, work on, and walk on. Many of us pay insufficient attention to our local landscape, especially when it's less than spectacular or pristine. And our focus is more often drawn to the flora and fauna, the man-made structures, and the other objects that may occupy the land rather than to the land itself.

The land is the earth's living, breathing skin. It's one of our planet's most vital organs, a life-giving, life-supporting, and in some respects fragile tissue that holds the weight of humanity with increasing difficulty. It's easily punctured and poisoned, and the ability of the land to regenerate and heal itself from our wounds is now becoming overwhelmed.

The land is the absolute ground of our existence and of all life. Almost everything that nourishes us comes from the land;

we, too, might as well have sprung right from the soil. Just as plants and trees won't survive if they're uprooted from the earth, neither will we flourish, or thrive spiritually, if we're disconnected from the land. We separate ourselves from it at our own peril. There's no life or future for us without land.

One of the first and easiest steps we can take to begin relating and reconnecting to the land is to start paying closer attention to it. No tract is too ordinary, too uninteresting, or too unimportant to be noticed and acknowledged—and respected—and appreciated. The most unassuming and homely little plot of land may conceal some extraordinary capabilities— namely the ability to give birth to an astonishing array of life-forms.

Even where it's been largely paved over, the land still breathes—although with considerable difficulty—and harbors life. In fertile areas where it's allowed to flourish unencumbered, the soil is absolutely saturated with life, including unimaginable numbers of microorganisms, insects, small mammals, fungi, plants, and the roots of trillions of trees.

Failing to connect with the land leaves us essentially homeless in the world. If we're unable to relate to the earth, we can never feel completely at ease in our habitat, whether or not we're conscious of it. Living in the finest house or apartment, or in the loveliest setting, can't begin to make up for it. Few things in life are lonelier than being alienated from the land.

Human beings were land-based creatures for a very long time, which may be why we require so much more than a suitable dwelling to feel at home here. Until recently, relating to the earth was vital to our lives and identities, and this remains reflected in the strong psychological and spiritual needs we have for contact with the land. Some of us suspect that achieving real wholeness and peace of mind may be impossible without it.

The Distinctiveness of the Local

Life is notable for its endless variety, and the same holds true for the land it flourishes on. Every area of land, when you get to know it, appears to possess a distinctive personality that distinguishes it from others; some call this particular feel or flavor the spirit of the place. Aside from obvious differences that exist between biologically and geologically dissimilar areas—high mountains and foothills, canyons and swamplands, rainforests and deserts—even within the most uniform of regions there's great local variability.

The hills, streams, trees, and other living things that may lie outside your window are by no means the same as those of your neighbors. There will surely be many similarities, but once we get to know the land, the differences often prove to be greater than we might have suspected. It's not unlike how the uniqueness of individual people and other creatures comes to life when we get to know them and become emotionally attached to them. When we develop an intimate relationship with an area of land, we're sure to discover its individuality as well.

Some people are able to travel widely and visit some of the planet's most magnificent natural landscapes. Whether or not we're so fortunate, it's important that we take the time to recognize and appreciate the specialness of our own little corner of the world. It's worth our while to uncover some of the hidden gifts of local lands. If you own, rent, or otherwise have easy access to an area of natural land, try setting the goal of getting to know every nook and cranny of it. Search for the land's seeming quirks or eccentricities, its subtleties and surprises, its pockets of serene or startling beauty, and notice how its characteristics may be related to those of other landscapes. And if you're so bold as to do so, consider making a vow to never take one speck of it for granted.

Connecting Ourselves with the Land

We need to find ways to actively link ourselves to the land. One of the best means of accomplishing this is to tend or care for it. This can be done through gardening, small-scale farming, growing other things, and restoring eroded or otherwise damaged areas. Such hands-on activities are usually satisfying pursuits in themselves, but they reward us most deeply by letting us directly interact with the land. They also allow us to give something back to it, which is something we too rarely do. The earth wouldn't be suffering so much nor the soil be so depleted if we could learn to give back more than a fraction of what we take. See if you can sense what the land requires and what labor you might contribute to help it heal from any past wounds.

Walking the land each day is another fruitful and therapeutic practice that helps connect us with the landscape. A walk can be useful and satisfying in a number of ways, including serving as a daily moving meditation on nature and the land. It can deepen our sense of relatedness to the living planet, strengthen the bonds we feel with the earth, and allow us to observe changes in the land from one day to the next, as well as over the course of weeks, months, seasons, years, and decades.

It's also important that we spend some time sitting quietly on the land. We can tune into the earth as well as our own inner state most easily when we're still. This is what meditation is all about. Although you can sit anywhere on the ground, look for an especially inviting spot that seems to call out for you to rest. You'll probably find some favorite places you'll want to return to again and again. Even your lawn may have a small hill or a sheltered site under a tree that feels especially comfortable. Return to this place regularly, especially anytime you're confused or stressed out. You can also try accessing it in your mind while indoors. If you so desire, such a locale can become a sort of entry point into the deeper recesses of the land that we've come to exclude ourselves from, a place where you can begin to explore and connect with the heart and soul of nature.

Notice how the ground feels to your body: soft or hard, smooth or rough, warm or cold, sensuous or uncomfortable. Pay attention to your inner sensations and feelings as well. Does the land seem like neutral, inert earth or like a cherished friend? Perhaps there's some other way to describe how you feel in its presence. Notice any changes in your perceptions or attitude over the course of months of regular contact with the land. Do you feel any regrets or sadness whenever it's time to go? For some of us it's like temporarily interrupting an important spiritual connection. But we can also keep the land alive and flourishing in our hearts and souls wherever we find ourselves.

Any tract that's in a reasonably unspoiled state should suffice for our efforts to relate to the land, including sitting, walking, and other land-based pursuits. Those of us who only have the smallest of lawns or unpaved plots can still adopt some of these activities. If we don't own or rent property, have a yard, or live near a natural area, it behooves us to seek out undeveloped lands at every available opportunity.

Letting the Land Lead Us

Take an experiential walk to get to know an area of land—either your own or one that's convenient or of interest to you. Such a walk can be done anywhere, including in an urban or suburban park. All you'll need for your walk is some "naked" land, unpaved and reasonably undeveloped. The ground could be bare, grassy, dense with vegetation, and/or forested; the surface might consist of soft dirt, sand, hard clay, or rock; and the terrain can be relatively flat, hilly, or steep.

Try to let the land lead you. Avoid trails or paths for this kind of walk—taking considerable care to not get lost if you're in a large natural area. Allow the contours of the land and the texture of the earth to guide you; drop any ideas or preconceptions about where you should go. Without thinking about it, you may find yourself moving in a particular direction or toward certain objects or elements and away from others. You'll probably be inclined to bypass large obstacles like boulders, possible hazards like drop-offs, and other impediments like mud or standing water.

Expect your attention to wander as you walk. Keep gently returning your focus to the land itself. What forms does it assume? Does the landscape have a particular feel to it? Are you reasonably at home here, or is there something that makes you feel uneasy or unsafe? Does the land evoke emotions or have any special meaning for you? If you can ignore for a moment what's growing on the surface, does the land itself seem to be alive to you?

Studying the Land

Examine all the elements that make up the land you live on or frequent, and try to find out as much as you can about their origins. Assuming you're physically able and feel sufficiently adventurous, explore thoroughly any landforms such as hills, depressions, cliffs, small canyons, ravines, caves, and rock formations. The shape of the landscape is the result of natural forces over the course of thousands or millions of years, including volcanic action, earthquakes, uplifting of the land, glaciation, or erosion. But much of what we see has been molded or affected as well by human intervention or habitation.

Old stone walls, rock piles, and building foundations are some of the more obvious signs of past human occupancy that may go back centuries. Sometimes these will be hidden by dense vegetation. Local histories may help you fill in the missing pieces, and reading or studying geology will increase your understanding of the forces that originally sculpted the natural landscape and continue to do so in ways that we only occasionally get a glimpse of, as during hurricanes and floods.

Examine closely any brooks, streams, rivers, and other waterways that traverse the land or area where you live. Try to track down their sources and final destinations, which could be a lake or an ocean. Valleys, ravines, and gullies that have streams running through them may have been carved by the coursing water.

Explore as well any lakes and ponds, as well as marshes and swamps. Are these ponds or lakes natural? If you can't find a dam, this is probably so. Are they fed by springs or streams?

You could study the soil as well. If you have a garden or otherwise grow any plants outdoors or indoors, or have ever been close to the world of farming, you may already know something about soil. Which plants are able to survive or flourish in an environment naturally depends in part upon the soil's often complex content, including its mineral richness and acidity.

An interesting project would be to take a census of the soil's visible inhabitants, including every plant you can identify. To do this for a large tract of land would be an enormously ambitious task, but on a small scale it's much more feasible. Try to figure out why some species are growing in one place rather than another. To what extent might the soil be the reason?

Caring for the Land

All land needs allies. Since human beings have done so much to harm the land, we have the greatest responsibility to help her heal. Start treating the land as you would your own body— or that of a friend or lover. The land needs your caretaking, your attention, and your respect. Tread lightly on her. Always show consideration. Don't dump on her or dig her up unnecessarily. Poisoning her in any way should be unspeakable and unthinkable.

It's not that we need to tiptoe around on her. The land can withstand a certain amount of human impact, and some of our interventions may even be helpful to her. There are times when we need to move some earth: to plant, to build, or to bury. The keys are respect, consideration, and restraint. We're entitled to do what's necessary to meet our basic needs. Beyond that, we should consider what's best for the land and its nonhuman inhabitants.

It's tragic to witness how the integrity of the land and the ecosystem it supports is so often disrupted or devastated by human actions. In this country it's often legal to bulldoze the land for a profit—at the total expense of the myriad nonhuman residents. In a more earth-respecting world, other living things might at least have some limited rights, including the right to live unmolested in a reasonably intact habitat. Although we're not currently forced by law to respect all other forms of life, we all surely have a deep ethical obligation to do so.

Listening to the Land

Humans are good at talking, doing, and dominating. We need to listen a lot more. The land often speaks quietly, except on those rare but momentous occasions when it shudders or shakes during an earthquake or spouts lava in a volcanic eruption. Most of the time it isn't shouting for our attention, and we have to make an effort to hear what the land may have to say.

How do we listen to the land? By spending quiet time there resting and observing. Granted, there's also room on the land for our constructive activities, social events, and celebrations. Many social activities are improved by holding them on the land rather than indoors, assuming there's a suitable setting and we're not trampling the vegetation or causing other harm; among the reasons for this are the healing presence of nature and the enlivening effects of contact with the earth.

But to attend fully and consciously to the land, we need to be alone or with quiet company. Try to tune into its energies while sitting, standing, or walking on the earth. Does the land speak or otherwise communicate with you? Does it make any of its needs known to you? Spend some time listening carefully. Be patient and keep your mind open; in time you'll hear something. The land speaks to those who are receptive.

11

❧

EMBRACING
UNBRIDLED LIFE

IT'S DIFFICULT TO GET our materially oriented minds around
the amazing phenomenon called life. And in spite of science's
long-standing efforts, we still know remarkably little about the
life process. One certainty is that life encompasses change, which
some of the security-minded among us are ambivalent about—
but others of us find exciting. Living matter is in a constant state
of flux: ever growing, being transformed, and dying.

When we look closely, life appears to be absolutely riddled
with mysteries. We may think we have an inkling of how it
works and where we've come from, but many puzzles and unan-
swerable questions remain. None of the explanations about how
we and the rest of the living universe got here seem entirely sat-
isfactory. All we have is the impressive evidence of life itself,
which is most spectacularly displayed in the natural world.

For too many modern people life is tragically empty and meaningless, a condition that's especially common in Western civilization. One solution, and a way to recover our lost sense of belonging and connectedness, is for us to reenter the forest of relationships found in nature—where we can come into communion with an extraordinary range of living beings and allow their life energies to infuse, inspire, and awaken us.

Attempting to Control Life

Human beings are notorious for their predilection for sorting, categorizing, and trying to control things. The need to control is a problem for a good many of us, who demonstrate a compulsion to direct other people's behavior and interfere with every natural process under the sun. The problem has gotten worse with our withdrawal from the natural world, and modern technologies have greatly magnified our potential to wreak havoc.

But life tends to resist being dominated, boxed, or controlled. Attempts to regiment life or put it on a leash frequently backfire. People rebel, and populations of organisms may multiply or otherwise behave unpredictably when they're manipulated. Most of us respond negatively, sometimes intensely so, to having our fates dictated by others. However, we do nevertheless internalize many familial and societal prescriptions and restrictions, some of which may be detrimental to us. Yet by stifling or otherwise failing to follow our deepest longings, we risk subverting our lives or straitjacketing our souls.

Our difficulty with accepting our own mortality and our feeling of powerlessness in the face of death are probably behind our need to control life. In this culture we're encouraged to do our utmost to deny death; our obsession with control may be an unconscious compensation. But if we have the courage to acknowledge and feel the vulnerability that comes with being alive—and to see that we can't force life to do what we want— it's possible that our need to control may start to melt away, and our ability to enjoy the limited time we have here may grow.

Those who are unwilling or unable to loosen their tight grip on life sometimes do considerable harm. More than a little of the larger-scale mischief-making and destruction we see taking place in the world today, whether it's war-making or selling off our precious natural resources, is perpetrated by people who seem power-and-control-obsessed. Implicated here are certain heads of state, many of our own political leaders, and the CEOs of some multinational corporations. It's clear that a self-serving, control-minded perspective is only possible among individuals who are truly alienated from the earth and who see themselves as totally separate from other human beings and the rest of creation. Such a mind-set can only arise among a people who have removed themselves physically, mentally, emotionally, and spiritually from their ancestral home in the natural world.

Being so divorced from nature further fuels the fears that underlie much of our need to dominate and control. We wouldn't fear death—or life—so intensely if our sustaining relationship with the natural world hadn't been severed, leaving us feeling lost in a seemingly uncaring universe. The therapy that might stand a chance of curing our condition is the one promoted throughout this book: we need to reconnect as completely as possible with the community of nature.

Letting Life Flourish

The life force surges strongly within most of us, which is evident throughout the living world. We carry inside us a will to survive, to create, and often to procreate. In some of us, however, these energies have become dormant or depressed, or are otherwise unexpressed. Getting in touch with these forces, paying close attention to them, and fully nurturing them can be extremely therapeutic and invaluable to us, and help each of us gain more complete entry into the natural parts of our own body and being.

If a person approaches life with an open mind and heart, the wonder of it all tends to shine brightly through. How could we ever fail to appreciate what an extraordinary process life is? Why do so few of us experience it as a miracle? Why doesn't ordinary life matter more to us? Why is it only during peak experiences— the birth of a baby, sexual union, or other transcendent moments—that we find ourselves flooded with the joy of being alive?

One of many possible answers is that life is sometimes painful and difficult, and our elation may be ambushed or subdued by our troubles. But life's discomforts tend to be most intensified when we're alienated from nature—when we don't understand the purpose of our existence or feel we really belong here. Growing up in dysfunctional families, which are one expression of our unbalanced world, leads many of us to go through life in an emotional fog. Emotional blockages are sure to keep the life force from flowing freely within and through us.

The curious condition we call life can also be frightening at times. Living requires courage. Some fear is inevitable, but it's least likely to rule us if we're connected with the earth and stay emotionally and spiritually grounded. The fact that we're all entirely mortal—that life is short and could end for us at any time, no matter how safe and healthy we may keep ourselves, or how young or old we may be—can actually be a great motivator for us. We can let our mortality be an incentive to avoid procrastinating and make the very most of life right now.

Achieving meaning and satisfaction involves more than merely setting goals or filling our time with activities. Finding personal fulfillment often seems to hinge on letting life unfold in a way that responds to our deepest desires, leanings, and longings. Best of all is when we allow life to progress within nature's purview. If we select nature as one of our teachers or mentors, we'll contribute further to our personal evolution and fulfillment and in the process perhaps receive some additional inspiration to carry on. Most important of all, from nature we can learn how to identify what's truly essential in life and how to make that count for us.

Waking Up Our Life Force

Passive, sedentary living allows our life force and spirit to languish. We're hardly likely to enjoy life or make much of a contribution to the world if we're lethargic or comatose. While rest has an essential place in any schedule, life also calls upon us to be active and interactive. In general, the less time we spend sitting in chairs, lapping up TV, and indulging in other activities that require minimal investment or involvement, the better. We should be moving our bodies around, especially outside, and doing things that interest and stimulate us.

All forms of physical activity and exercise will help arouse and intensify our life energies as long as they're done in meaningful, nonmechanical, nonobsessive, and not overly routinized ways that allow for some spontaneity and freedom of movement. All the outdoor and nature-based activities we discussed in Chapters 6 and 7 are appropriate, as are any other self-propelled activities we may be attracted to.

The right kind of exercise that's done in the right way feels wonderful to us. This isn't simply because the body is temporarily overrun with endorphins. Exercise and activity have the healthful effect of stimulating many natural processes in the body, including improving circulation, sensory acuity, and the functioning of the brain. In turn, our creativity is enhanced and our abilities to think clearly and problem-solve are sharpened. Best of all, we may feel utterly and intensely alive, as confirmed by the sensations in our glowing, tingling bodies; it's as if our life force is on fire. Such an energetic aliveness can affect every aspect of our existence.

Almost any activity we carry out with pleasure and that involves at least a modicum of vigor, passion, or intense interest is likely to stimulate our life force. This can occur with dancing, cycling, singing, and even washing the car or painting the house. Having lively, engaged, and meaningful conversations with other people may have a similar result as well, as can interacting with other living beings in nature. When we spend enough time in the natural world, in fact, swimming in that ocean of life seems to affect our life force by osmosis; it's impossible to avoid absorbing the vibrant energies of other living things.

Experiencing Life in the Raw

A completely domesticated life may give the appearance of comfort and contentment, which it does indeed sometimes possess. But it can also teeter on the brink of boredom, emotional flatness, sedentary enervation, or the tedium that may come from living in an excessively predictable way. Being totally domesticated can mean being perpetually under control, reflecting a lack of inner freedom and a severely diminished spirit and soul.

Visits to wild nature remind us of life's potentiality, infinite richness, and soulfulness. Few things are more interesting and exciting to those of us who are receptive to it than the vision of raw, fresh, lovely, unprocessed, uncontrolled life that comprises so much of unspoiled nature. It seems there's almost no limit to what we can gain by rubbing elbows with such an incredible assortment of other living, breathing beings.

To be in the presence of wild nature is almost always stimulating and stirring. The effect could hardly be otherwise considering the congregation of life amassed there. Throughout the more fertile areas and seasons the natural landscape is absolutely flooded with living energies. The controls on life here come largely from interrelationships and ecological limits rather than from inner restraints.

Granted it may take some time for our often weary or anesthetized senses to fully absorb, feel, or even recognize nature's smorgasbord of energies, given that most life-forms don't advertise themselves or shout to get our attention the way our media and the rest of the man-made world do. Plants are quiet and stationary, and most wildlife keep their distance when we pass through, so it's easy for an outsider to get the false impression that life is subdued in nature.

In spite of all the seemingly mind-expanding elements of our high-tech civilization, the truth is that by shutting out nature and dwelling so exclusively in the human domain, we've in some respects narrowed our focus and stunted our consciousness. By spending time in the wild and exposing ourselves to the greater, more expansive sphere of life, we may find our awareness, our consciousness, and even our ability to feel radically expanded.

This doesn't mean that humanity necessarily becomes any less interesting or fascinating to us. And going in a more natural direction by no means requires that we start giving precedence to other species over the needs and concerns of our own. We have every right to take good care of ourselves, and it's truly unfortunate that vital human needs go unmet for many. These neglected needs, in fact, include the very one addressed here: our need to connect with other living things.

Undomesticating Ourselves

To the extent that our souls and spirits have been tamed, restricted, or chained, we need to expose them to hefty doses of fresh air and allow them to run free more often. We need to loosen ourselves from any emotional or spiritual bindings—to let go of overly narrow perspectives and attitudes, addictions to comfort and predictability, and fears of the unknown, all of which limit our lives. We can let wild nature show us the way.

Undomesticating ourselves doesn't mean giving ourselves license to behave irresponsibly, regressing to behavior harmful to others or ourselves, abandoning goals or aspirations, dismissing our education or manners, or giving up on our values. It means being willing to consider discarding some of our preconceived notions regarding what life may be about and how we're supposed to live, and greatly reducing any limits we've imposed on ourselves. At the same time, we're invited to recognize the preciousness and sacredness of the life impulse, and we're encouraged to empathize and identify with the extraordinary array of other beings through which this force is expressed.

Nature and wilderness can teach us some but not all of what we need to know about becoming less domesticated and freeing ourselves from the more harmful bounds and bondages of civilization. Human beings are unique in certain respects, as are so many of life's other manifestations. We're less instinct-driven and more culture-dependent than other animals, and we can't mimic other species to find our way. We must, rather, attempt to uncover the wildness that's hiding within ourselves.

Appreciating and Celebrating Life

Life and nature call for appreciation, gratitude, and also for celebration. Our load in life is lightened when we regularly find something to appreciate and be thankful for both in and out of nature. It shouldn't be hard for us to see that we indeed have a great deal to be grateful for. Just to be alive is a fantastic gift. If it's not easy for you to express gratitude either inwardly or out-wardly, take the time to cultivate such a practice. Life becomes more pleasurable and our problems appear to shrink in magnitude when we truly feel and can communicate a deep appreciation for what we've been given.

Something else is seriously missing if we don't also include celebration in our lives. Where's the evidence that existence was intended to be a grim and humorless business? It's easy to feel, in fact, that joy and enjoyment are what life was made for. When we have fun and celebrate, any difficulties we've encountered usually seem well worth the trouble. Few things are better for our mental health; celebrating helps dissipate stress and rebalance our internal world. And it puts us squarely in the present moment, which is where we properly belong. It makes sense to practice celebrating as often as possible, alone as well as with others, and both in and out of nature. Simply visiting the natural world puts some of us in a celebratory mood, and we shouldn't postpone acting on the urge. See how many life-and nature-affirming festivities you can come up with.

12

Rediscovering Our Place in the Universe

We belong on this beautiful planet. There's truly a place for us in the scheme of things here, assuming we can refrain from wrecking our inheritance. This sacred earth is the only real home we'll ever have, as will be true for untold generations of our descendants—and all of creation's other progeny—as long as our sun keeps burning and life endures. And it's clear that at our core we're still natural beings, who in order to flourish and fulfill our destinies require a network of physical, emotional, and spiritual relationships with the rest of the living world.

Yet collectively we've been losing touch with our natural selves, assisted by our aggressively materialistic culture, which coaxes and manipulates us into ignoring our natural inclinations. We're dissuaded from listening to or respecting our deepest inner leanings. And we've forgotten many of the basic truths and requirements of living that our ancestors knew and that some remaining indigenous peoples still honor. Many of us no longer know who we are or why we're here. As individuals, some of us do still manage to find meaning, passion, and purpose in our lives, but millions of others among us have lost their bearings in the universe.

We've never been more on our own than now when it comes to locating our place in life. Society once offered extensive guidance on how to live; this admittedly had a negative side, namely that roles were sometimes too narrowly defined and prescriptions too strictly dictated. Today, finding purpose is largely an individual, personal pursuit. A search for meaning may be precipitated by a serious crisis in our lives, or it may be part of a lifelong quest. Either way, our rudderless culture provides us with little assistance in addressing and answering the deeper questions.

Not surprisingly, some powerful remedies for our dislocation and disorientation can be found in the natural world, the communal realm we've so thoroughly separated ourselves from. If we're willing to start listening to nature again and be patient, some of the solutions to our problems will start to crystallize for us. In time, we may learn how to better orient ourselves in the universe, navigate our way through the minefields of the modern world, reinvest our existence with meaning, and find the paths that lead toward what's most valuable in life.

Membership in the Earth Community

One of the most important things we learn from nature—which echoes many religious and spiritual teachings—is that we're not separate from the rest of creation. It's a misperception to see ourselves as entirely independent or isolated beings. Ecology repeatedly confirms this, revealing our myriad interconnections with the lives of other species, whose well-being often directly or indirectly affects our own. When we understand that we're physically and spiritually enfolded within a complex web of life, it is hard to feel lost or lonely.

We belong to an earth community, whether we fully acknowledge and accept it or not. It's the most diverse assembly imaginable, consisting of every manner and variety of being that inhabits our planet. We must never forget or lose sight of the fact that we can't survive without this larger community. The fantasies of some futurists notwithstanding, if the earth became barren of life other than our own it would be an uninhabitable place, a soulless wasteland.

Membership in any community bestows benefits as well as confers obligations. We gain in innumerable ways from the presence of our floral and fauna relatives, each of whom fills a particular niche and makes some contribution to our ecosystem. The sum of these inputs creates the living world we exist in and through which we fulfill our needs. Thus it's only appropriate that we attempt to keep this community in as healthy a state as possible, and also give something back.

Awareness of our membership in the earth community affects our thoughts and perceptions as well as our behavior. It enables us to see networks of interspecies connections and relationships that may have previously been invisible to us. The feeling many people now have of being alone in the world is completely contradicted by a look at the larger life community, although many of civilization's practices do foster a greater sense of isolation. The increasing fragmentation and dissolution of human communities and the lack of community many people experience in their everyday lives are well-known characteristics of modern life in the Western world. And while as social beings we need to have meaningful contact with other people, we should also enter and find companionship within the widest circles of life. If we do so, any feelings we have of loneliness, separation, or isolation should soon evaporate.

How do we learn to approach and interact with the greater community of life? And how do we rediscover where we belong within the natural order? There's no one simple set of steps for each of us to follow, but as discussed earlier in this book, the stronger our desire to find our way back into relationship with nature, and the more time we're willing and able to spend in the wild, the more probable it is that we'll be rewarded. It's in nature that we'll become reacquainted with our natural selves and renew our membership in the community of life.

Living in a World of Limits

Among the lessons we learn from sitting at nature's side is that life and the earth are fragile in many ways, and the world we occupy has very finite physical limits. These facts are extremely important and should be considered whenever we make choices. They totally contradict the misleading messages we receive from the advertising world, which assure us that we can have anything we want and urge us to indulge our every whim.

The unfortunate consequences of unrestrained consumerism on the earth haven't been obvious to most of us until recently. The truth, which is becoming increasingly apparent, is that our purchases have a pronounced impact on life and the environment, extending far beyond what we would imagine to be our personal sphere of influence. The long-term effects of taking more than we need include accelerating the destruction of irreplaceable natural resources, contributing to the undermining of our planet's health, and leaving future generations with a faltering ecosystem.

But the fact that we live in a physical universe with many vulnerabilities and built-in limits need not be discouraging or bad news. Life still allots us a great amount of freedom, and we're left with a host of interesting choices. The natural order and inherent structures of life also offer us a much-needed framework within which to act and live out our lives. Embracing this order can increase our sense of security, the value of which shouldn't be underestimated in a world that seems to be coming apart at the seams.

Also, from a psychological and emotional standpoint, attempting to satisfy our every whim and desire is far from a fulfilling way to live—this is age-old wisdom. The pleasures of constant self-indulgence quickly wear thin and take us far afield from true satisfaction. For the sake of optimizing both our physical and mental health, living in moderation makes the most sense. Acting thoughtfully and responsibly, which includes exercising restraint when appropriate, has the added benefit of putting us on a path of integrity—with a number of positive consequences for us and our integrity-starved world.

Assuming Responsibility for the Earth

Our responsibility to respect natural limits and refrain from damaging the earth helps define one of our most important roles as human beings. To the extent that each of us is capable of doing so, we're called upon to be caretakers and protectors of the planet, and we should demonstrate through our actions our concern for all of life. Never before has taking on the responsibility of stewardship been more vital, because never before has the planet been so jeopardized by the destructive actions of one species, namely our own. This shouldn't feel like we're taking on a weighty or oppressive obligation. To the contrary, if we go about it in the right frame of mind it can be enormously satisfying to work for life's sake and to give something back to the earth, which contributes to the well-being of humanity as well.

The earth needs few things more right now than for concerned citizens to take a stand and help defend her. One person can make a real difference, as has been repeatedly demonstrated by individuals who have succeeded in rallying the public behind environmental and other causes. If you don't think you have the time, energy, or inclination to get involved in such activities, you can still help by contacting your political and other leaders and urging them to take earth-protecting actions. You should also join and support environmental, conservation, and wilderness preservation groups. It's essential, too, that we all do our absolute best to live in a way that's respectful of the planet. Resolve to avoid unnecessary purchases, tread carefully on the earth, and if you're about to raise a family, consider helping limit population growth by having no more than one child. Such efforts can help bring life back into balance.

Learn more about the places you visit when you commune with nature, whether they're national, state, or local parks, forests, sanctuaries, reservations, preserves, or other natural areas. Some of these locations are likely to be well-protected and well-maintained, but others may be neglected or at risk of being sold and developed. Every year large tracts of wild land are bulldozed and turned into malls, golf courses, or sprawling housing developments. Local environmental protection groups can keep you informed of areas that are currently endangered. Your interest and willingness to speak up can make a real difference when such lands are at risk of being denatured. Consider "adopting" a tract that needs defending or other assistance. Maybe you could volunteer to help publicize the problem or perhaps aid in restoring lands that are already damaged.

Discovering Our Purpose

Who are we? Why are we here? Each of us must answer such questions in our own way. Some of us are fortunate to have a solid, healthy sense of self and a clear sense of purpose or calling in life, which is truly a gift in these troubled times. Maybe we were lucky enough to have been born into a family that encouraged us to uncover our purpose, or we may have had to search or even struggle to find it on our own. Or, like so many others, perhaps we're still at a loss to know what our purpose is. We may even find it impossible to believe any such purpose exists.

The advantages of having a purpose should be self-evident; it's usually empowering, gives our life direction, allows us to be more effective in the world, and enables us to use our time and energy much more economically. Assuming we have indeed discovered, gleaned, or otherwise become aware of a purpose for living, to what extent does it encompass the universe at large? Rarely is one's purpose merely a personal matter, without consequences to others or the earth. If we're not sure how our purpose fits into the bigger picture, it's worth exploring the possible planetary ramifications of our beliefs and behaviors.

While no one can or should attempt to impose a purpose on someone else, it's impossible to ignore some of the purposes that life and nature seem to invite us to entertain and perhaps internalize. These include doing everything in our power to foster and encourage all forms of life, as well as helping to create and maintain a planetary environment where species are permitted to flourish unencumbered, amid adequate space and healthy, nontoxic conditions. Accomplishing such goals appears to require discouraging the procreation and reducing the population of our species, as we've already greatly exceeded ecological limits and taken over much of the land needed by other species. We may need to collectively strive for a planetary maximum of perhaps two billion people, which would be environmentally sustainable over the long run if we can simultaneously learn to live in more earth-honoring ways.

Open your ears, eyes, and other senses widely in nature's presence and you'll receive other suggestions for enhancing life on this vibrant earth. Perhaps you'll achieve insights that will lead you to discover or develop a planetary purpose and vision that could have far-reaching implications. Each of us needs to find our own way on this earth, which in no way precludes sharing the experience or collaborating with others in our efforts. And although outcomes aren't totally predictable, there's a very real possibility that our lives will flower and be transformed in the process.

PART II

COMMUNING
WITH NATURE

13

∞

TOUCHING THE EARTH

ALTHOUGH LIFE ORIGINATED in the seas, it's been rooted in the moist, fertile earth for many millions of years. And until the modern era, the physical face of the planet provided the stage upon which most of humanity's stories were played out. Since the majority of us have now relocated to more artificial settings, we've lost the intimacy we once had with the rich, life-giving soil. We're now literally out of touch with the earth.

Chapter 5 discussed the importance of grounding ourselves on the earth, and Chapter 10 examined the broader qualities and characteristics of the land. This chapter will take a look at the material ingredients that constitute the earth itself, including soil, mud, sand, and rock, which may or may not be covered with vegetation. Their stature is somewhat humble when compared with nature's more conspicuous and imposing displays, and they'll often elude our notice as we pass by, but these root elements nevertheless deserve our attention and appreciation.

Soil

It's interesting to note some of the negative connotations the words *dirt* and *soil* carry, which reflects a "civilized" point of view. This is another expression of our alienation from nature, as well as an example of the negativity we habitually project onto the earth. As any gardener or farmer knows, however, few substances on the planet are ultimately more precious than healthy soil or dirt. Much of life simply couldn't exist without this vital mix of organic matter. Let the soil deteriorate and watch life languish; let it erode away and watch life disappear.

To really get to know the soil, we need to actually poke around in it and run some of it through our hands. A closer look may reveal myriad signs of life, some of which will require a magnifying glass to reveal, including the menagerie of tiny creatures that permeate and help vitalize the soil, as well as the root hairs of many varieties of vegetation. Where we haven't already dug or plowed it up, and where it hasn't been stirred up or tunneled into by our fellow creatures, the soil tends to be harder and more compact when dry—whereas moist or well-watered ground is naturally softer and much more likely to be covered by a mantle of green grass or other vegetation.

We should always be respectful in our earthy explorations and remember that any digging we do, no matter how limited, means we're taking a bite out of the habitat and disrupting whatever beings may live there—restraint and care are called for. It takes a very long time for soil to regenerate when we remove it; countless generations of living things are required to contribute the organic matter that makes up this vital substance. In places where the growing season is short, this process takes many hundreds of years or more. In fragile or protected areas, including most parks and wilderness areas, it's usually unethical and also illegal to dig or otherwise alter the landscape in any way.

In less natural areas, where the land has been heavily impacted by human development or other interventions, we can do many things to help improve the soil, assuming the land is ours or we're otherwise permitted to take such actions. In some areas the soil has been depleted by past farming practices, for example, or poisoned by chemical fertilizers or lawn treatments. Along with avoiding any future use of toxic pesticides or herbicides, among the beneficial actions we can take is to compost and contribute organic matter to the earth.

In wild nature we'll periodically find places where some digging has already been done for us, as when we come upon a small pile of fresh dirt next to a hole in the ground, most likely from an animal digging or enlarging a tunnel, burrow, or den. We can also frequently find some loose, exposed soil alongside eroded riverbanks and stream banks. To minimize our impact on the natural environment, we should be on the lookout for such locations and examine the excavated soil there rather than intrusively digging on our own.

When considering the world of nature, the importance of the soil is easily overlooked, given its limited visibility and the presence of so many other interesting elements and inhabitants that are continually competing for our attention. We shouldn't lose sight of how essential the soil is for the nourishment and survival of so many living things, including the endless array of attractive flora. Without this moist, mineral-rich bed of life-sustaining matter the natural realm would be a barren place, and most creatures, ourselves included, would find their food sources missing and their ability to survive challenged.

Studying the Soil

Look for some loose soil you can get your hands into, or use a stick to dig a small hole. Do this in your yard or any other location where it's legal, there's ample soil, and you won't be defacing the landscape or harming vegetation. You'll also want to avoid potentially toxic locations. Be wary of roadsides or ditches, for example, where dangerous chemicals might have been dumped sometime in the past. Take any unnatural, unpleasant smell as a possible tip-off and your cue to move on.

Place some freshly uncovered soil in your hands and study it closely, with or without a magnifying glass. Do an inventory of what you find, while simultaneously noticing your own responses. Can you find any insects or other little critters moving around? Are there small roots or other signs of vegetation? Take a bit of time and try to be patient; some dirt discoveries will be so tiny or subtle that identifying them can be a challenge.

Notice how moist or dry and how soft or hard the soil is. Does it have a detectable scent? Are there stones or rock fragments within it? Digging may be difficult in a rocky area. If you've taken soil from near the surface of the ground, go a little deeper if you can and notice what, if anything, changes with the depth. Do you come across any air spaces or cavities? There's always a chance that you'll dig into a tunnel or burrow belonging to a rodent, reptile, or other creature. Vast networks of such tunnels exist underground, and not all of them are currently occupied; your chances of encountering any sizable residents are slim.

When you're finished, be sure to replace whatever dirt you may have removed, and try to erase all traces of your excavation. Repeat this elsewhere, noticing the similarities and differences in the soil. Does this interesting, life-enhancing substance start to have any more meaning for you? Do you have a sense of how what goes on beneath the surface may eventually affect what transpires above ground and elsewhere in the world, including within your own body? Can you connect in some way with these "dirty" yet life-sustaining elements and processes?

Mud

The earth doesn't get much dirtier or messier than when it takes the form of mud, which is the main reason why so few of us feel affection for this particular planetary element. Most children clearly are exceptions, however, and they seem to instinctively know how to have fun in it. Many of us can remember playing in the stuff and making mud pies when we were kids, and we may have gotten in trouble with our parents for it. Some other creatures are drawn to mud for different reasons, including for the moist, cool environment that moderates summer heat. Those of us who are obsessed with cleanliness may find mud intolerable; keeping footwear clean in it is clearly impossible.

Since soil plus water equals mud, we can usually count on finding plenty of the mucky stuff during rainy seasons— especially in the spring, following the melting of winter snows. Those of us who walk or hike on dirt paths and trails in areas with significant precipitation are sure to encounter it. But we can often skirt areas where the mud is deep, and planks or boardwalks are sometimes provided in and around swamps, marshes, bogs, and other areas that stay wet or muddy most of the year.

A good pair of hiking boots will go a long way toward minimizing mud problems. Since boots by definition are at least ankle-high (anything cut below the ankle is a shoe), they'll successfully protect our feet from most mud, rocks, and other earth elements. Higher boots are necessary for dealing with deeper mud, but regular-size hiking or other outdoor boots should be more than adequate for handling the amount of mud most of us will ordinarily encounter. They'll need to be cleaned off afterward of course, but this is truly a minor chore.

Taking a Barefoot Mud Walk

If you're willing to defy convention, don't mind getting your feet dirty, and want to have a bit of fun, a barefoot mud walk may be for you. Yes, you're at serious risk of being considered eccentric by any passersby as well as by your friends. Yet getting some of your body into the mud can actually be quite a pleasurable and sensual experience, as most kids already know. It'll almost certainly leave you feeling friendlier toward and maybe even at one with this particular element, and possibly allow you to be more at home elsewhere in the ungroomed and sometimes untidy world of nature. Your main task when getting started is to keep any negative preconceptions or expectations from getting in the way.

Enjoy the moist, mushy feel of the mud on your bare feet and ankles as you sink in with each step. Be ready to backtrack or keep to the side if it gets too deep. As with other barefoot walking or wading in a lake, there's always a slight chance you could cut your foot on a sharp stick, rock, or any other concealed object; to minimize that risk, step down carefully. You could try turning your walk into a mud meditation: go slowly and visually follow the motion of your feet through the mud, while allowing your mind to sink into a softer, earthier state.

Sand

Probably few of us can claim to be seasoned mud-walkers, whereas almost all of us have enjoyed walking barefoot in the sand at a beach. For many of us, summers in childhood meant regular trips to the shore, which some of us continue to enjoy as adults. Besides memories of swimming and sunning ourselves, we can probably remember well the pleasures of walking in wet sand along the shoreline near lapping waves or roaring surf. We may also recall the sting of hot, dry sand on the bottoms of our bare feet. Our sensory memories of sand are likely to be vivid.

Sand seems to have been especially made for children, which is why sandboxes have long been provided in playgrounds. It's malleable and movable, and—as with mud or clay—when it's wet, you can make or build things with it. But sand doesn't lose its appeal as we grow older, and few of us can resist walking, exploring, and messing around with it when we're at the beach. Dry sand shows few signs of life at first glance, but a closer look will sometimes reveal insects and other diminutive beings carrying on. Away from the shoreline we're likely to find an assortment of vegetation taking root in the substance.

Beach sand is ever on the move, especially in and around the water. The constant lapping or pounding of waves, which is most pronounced during storms, shifts and bulldozes enormous amounts of sand, creates and deletes sandbars, and moves or washes away entire beaches. Sand is also tossed around by brisk winds. No beach stays the same for long, which is one well-publicized reason why it's so unwise to build a house close to the water.

During a leisurely day at the beach, some of us are sure to find ourselves studying the sand—peering closely at the particles and grains, running them through our hands, perhaps letting them stir our thoughts and imaginations, and pondering their origins as well as our own. Contemplating the sand tends to remind us of the passage of enormous, mind-bending amounts of time. It's difficult to believe this substance could really be the pulverized remains of rocks—the result of millions of years of battering against each other and weathering by water.

Not all sand is located near lakes or the sea. There are many inland areas with sandy soil far from any current bodies of water, evidence that an ocean or lake presumably existed there at some time in the distant past. This, too, may provoke in us thoughts about the unimaginable amounts of time that have passed prior to our arrival on the scene and how extremely short-term, in comparison, our own stay here will be.

Rock

Major portions of our planet are comprised of rock. This hardest of natural substances underlies much of the earth's surface and rises above us in the forms of mountains, rock formations, and other geological features (see Chapter 18). Boulders, smaller rocks, stones, gems, and other fractured and weathered fragments are widely scattered on the ground as well as buried beneath it. The origins of rock are multiple and diverse, and the shapes and forms it can take seem to be limitless.

In spite of the incredible hardness of most rock and how difficult it is for us to break it, the actions of water and weather over time slowly and inexorably wear it away. Wintertime and cold temperatures accelerate the damage, as water in cracks freezes and expands when it turns to ice; the enormous pressure generated is sometimes sufficient to split or fracture the rock.

Aside from the high mountains, spectacular canyons, and rock formations we may visit on our vacations, most rocks we encounter tend to be of the ordinary, unassuming sort that are easily overlooked. Sometimes we don't notice them until we trip over them. It's easy to take for granted the everyday variety of rocks, such as those that make up the old stone wall running alongside our property, the occasional rock that's kicked up while we're mowing the lawn, or the gravel in our driveway or alongside the nearest highway. Once in a while, though, when sitting by a clear stream we'll notice some beautifully smooth stones under the water and feel the urge to pick some of them up and look them over. Or we may perk up upon sighting some precious gems in a store window or on a bracelet.

Many indigenous cultures believe rocks have spirits and are alive, whereas relatively few in our society learn to perceive them in such ways. Yet rocks actually feed all living things through the life-sustaining minerals they gradually release into the soil. These hardy "beings" also contribute a solidity and a sense of timelessness to our physical universe. When we see a large boulder perched on a cliff or sitting alone in an open field, we can guess that it was probably moved there by an ice-age glacier many millennia ago; in its life span, this is mere seconds. Nothing we know of will outlive a rock.

Going Rock Hunting

Take a rock walk. Let your primary purpose be locating rocks of all kinds, sizes, and descriptions, from little stones to giant boulders. Some will be prominent alongside the trail, while others will be well-concealed by vegetation or buried in the soil. If you're in a public park or other protected area, don't disturb the soil by digging up rocks and removing them. There's no harm, however, in moving around some loose rocks in a streambed or skipping stones across the surface of a pond.

Collecting and taking home rocks, stones, and other natural items is usually forbidden on public lands for good reason; if enough people take these and other elements, the environment will eventually be stripped of its natural beauty and constituent parts. As with other natural items, try to get to know the rocks where they are. If you do move them, show respect before you leave by returning them to the approximate place where you found them.

Don't hesitate to touch and feel rocks with your hands. Pick up any loose stone or rock that's not too heavy and examine it closely. Enjoy the tactile sensations, noticing whether the rock is rough or smooth, and whether the shape is irregular or relatively symmetrical. Does it have sharp edges that suggest it may have recently broken off from a larger rock? Or are the edges and corners smooth as if they've been immersed in water for a long time? Does the rock have colors or distinctive patterns? Is a fossil visible, by any chance? If so, can you guess what kind of creature it might have been?

Reading about geology can increase our knowledge and understanding of where rocks come from, how they're formed, how old they may be, and how the various kinds differ from each other. Just as it's helpful to know something about flora and fauna when we're exploring the wild, a rock walk becomes more interesting when we're able to tentatively identify the rocks we encounter and have some idea about their origins.

Before heading home, consider spending some time sitting quietly with a favorite rock. Think about this ancient natural object and meditate on it if you like. Does its solidity suggest anything to you? If it could speak, might it have something to say to you? Does it evoke a particular feeling for you? Does it impress or inspire you in any way? If you could speak directly to it—this is, of course, within your power to do if you're so inclined—what would you want to say to this earthly elder?

Other Elements Underfoot

Substantial areas of the earth's surface are covered with vegetation, and whenever we spend time in nature we'll often find ourselves walking, standing, sitting, or lying on such living things as tree roots, grass, and other flora. While most trails or paths in natural areas are relatively clear of vegetation, and they are sometimes routed to bypass fragile species, there's usually no way to avoid stepping on flora altogether since they're everywhere in nature. Without being overly anxious about it, we should simply do our best to trample them as little as possible.

Walking on tree roots doesn't harm them at all, and in forested areas (see Chapters 15 and 17) exposed roots are frequently everywhere underfoot. On some unimproved trails and paths, you may be constantly stepping on or over them; be careful and attentive to avoid tripping. Be aware as well that roots can be extremely slippery and hazardous when wet, so proceed especially cautiously in rainy weather.

It's worth stopping to study the root systems where they're visible, which is sometimes the result of erosion. In wet terrain we'll sometimes find toppled trees with much of their root systems elevated in the air, fully exposed for our convenient examination. We may also come upon small trees perched on top of rocks or boulders, seemingly growing right out of them, although their roots usually reach down around the rocks to connect with some soil below.

Grass

Grass is obviously the variety of vegetation we're most likely to find ourselves walking on, and many of us have it growing right outside our door. As we presumably know, we won't hurt grass simply by walking across it; only when we repeatedly trample it or shield it from the sun is it harmed or killed. We need not be shy about roaming around in grass, but at the same time we should avoid deliberately walking on unidentified grasses in the wild. Some of them could be rare and endangered species.

The grasses we've planted in our lawns and that we find in most public parks are extremely homogeneous. And we're in the habit of keeping them closely cropped, which greatly limits the opportunities for other life-forms, including wildlife. Our yards would be much more interesting and naturally attractive if we allowed other kinds of grasses and vegetation to take root and let them grow to their natural height. One of the few advantages of a short-grass lawn is that everything's totally visible, so we can walk or run around barefoot without having to watch for hazards. Most of us know well what it's like to walk barefoot around our lawn or at a lakeside park. Next time you do this, try turning it into a full-blown sensory experience for your feet by tuning into and feasting on the range of sensations.

Getting Down in the Grass

Whether or not you've been engaging in some grass-walking, barefoot or otherwise, sit down and stretch out in the grass. Start out by lying on your stomach or side, and see what you can discover within and under the green growth. Examine the blades of grass closely, and look for other plants that may share the area, such as clover, dandelions, and other members of that enormous community of often overlooked plants we prefer to call weeds. At the same time, watch for insects and other tiny creatures that may be crawling around on the grass or in the soil, such as worms, caterpillars, beetles, and other bugs. Are any of them familiar to you? Do you know their common or scientific names? In cool or cold weather there will be less to see, whereas during the warmer months the ground should be alive with small-scale activity.

When you've had your fill of exploring and investigating, roll over on your back, or assume any other position you might favor and shift your body to get as comfortable as possible. Try to fully relax and feel the grass pressing against any exposed skin. Is your overall feeling a pleasurable one? Is there something reassuring about being here? If you have the time and are willing to stay put, spend as much as a couple of hours deeply immersed in the world of grass, with its plush, green carpet of small plants and curious, diminutive creatures. Enjoy the ever-reliable support of the earth beneath your body and the soft, intimate embrace of so many living beings.

14

❧

Going with the
Flow of Water

Water is the lubricant of life. Most living things are utterly
infused with it. By weight our moist bodies consist mainly of
water, as does our food. Without replenishing our reserves, none
of us can survive for more than a few days. It's no accident that
we find fresh, clean water to be such a thirst-quenching drink or
that liquid refreshments play an important role at so many of
our social events.

Not surprisingly, the water we encounter in nature in the
form of streams, rivers, waterfalls, ponds, lakes, and oceans is
irresistibly attractive to most of us—as it appealingly laps, ripples, sprays, and sparkles in the sun. We take delight in the very
same substance that comprised the ancient seas where life began.
Water can be seen as the original womb of life.

Our response to the sounds made by moving water in a natural setting is equally positive. These are among the most relax-

ing and mesmerizing sounds we know of. In warmer weather many of us can't refrain from getting our bodies into the stuff— to swim, splash around, wade, or at least soak our feet. Much of our motivation is usually to cool off or clean up, but even in cold weather water tends to draw us like a powerful magnet.

Those who have grown up amid civilization's sadly polluted waters may find it amazing or even unbelievable to witness clear, clean, delicious water flowing directly from the earth or cradled in a placid, pristine lake. Thankfully there are still protected waters that run reasonably pure. If anything in creation is sacred, it surely must be such life-giving waters.

Brooks, Creeks, Streams, and Rivers

The sights and sounds of water flowing in nature quickly and consistently capture our attention. Our usual impulse upon first becoming aware of a nearby stream or river is to make a beeline for it. We're attracted to the moving water, which excites and seems to energize us. Especially inspiring are the larger rivers, which carry massive volumes of water great distances to the sea. Yet even the smallest brook or stream can be extremely charming and enticing. We may want to poke around along the banks or simply sit down to watch, listen, and rest. Even when we know a waterway well, we'll often be inclined to pay regular return visits.

Because so many people are drawn to waterways and can't resist exploring them, natural streams and creeks frequently have primitive paths running alongside them. Sometimes there'll be a designated nature, hiking, or multiuse trail. Such trails are most common in popular parks and other accessible natural areas, whereas in wilder and more remote places we may have to make our own way. Larger rivers that lie outside of wilderness areas are often followed by roads or highways, which usually preclude the possibility of quiet solitude. For a more restful experience we may want to seek out smaller creeks and streams that are away from roads.

Chapter 6 addressed a number of outdoor recreational activities including canoeing, kayaking, and rafting. These are all superb means of enjoying waterways that are large and deep enough to float watercraft. Aside from the adventure and fun involved, you can cover considerable distances and explore much more scenery than on foot, including through areas where the riverbanks are too rugged or steep for walking. You move with the water itself, which lifts you out of a land-based mind-set for a time. Aside from the requirement of owning, borrowing, or renting a canoe or kayak, and the need to be skilled in paddling and navigating it, the only other drawback is that you'll miss out on some more ground-based perspectives and riverbank minutiae.

Exploring a Waterway on Foot

Whether or not a trail or path is available, it's interesting and enjoyable to follow a creek, stream, or river on foot for some distance. There's little risk of getting lost as long as you keep the water in sight, and when you're ready to go back, simply return the way you came. If the water's low or there's a bridge, you also have the option of crossing and coming back on the other side. Waterways in mountain regions and other natural areas sometimes run through rough terrain. If it's rocky, go slowly and be extra careful to avoid tripping or stumbling—which could result in a twisted ankle—or slipping and falling on a wet rock.

You may find the moving, "talking" water inviting you to stop or pause frequently to view each bend of the brook and listen to the singing or murmuring sounds. If you're intent on covering some ground, you'll probably want to resist stopping often, but sometimes it's also tempting to drop whatever agenda you have and stay put in one place, which has the benefit of allowing you to get to know a small stretch of stream thoroughly. See how many fish, tadpoles, frogs, crabs, and other aquatic creatures you can find. Along quiet stretches you'll frequently see water striders, the skating bugs that dart back and forth across the water's surface. Check out the vegetation as well. Often diverse plant life can be found growing by the water and sometimes in or under it.

It's pleasurable to watch the water wend its way along, twisting and turning, swirling and bubbling around rocks and other barriers, churning and foaming over rapids, speeding up between obstacles and along straightaways, and slowing down where it enters pools. While it may not exactly compete with the high-tech entertainment we have available to us back at home, communing with water can be a surprisingly engrossing and enjoyable way to spend downtime. Whiling away a few afternoon hours by a beautiful mountain stream is precisely the kind of easy, natural pursuit that enables our overloaded brains and nervous systems to downshift into a more restful, low-key, restorative mode that may leave us feeling utterly serene.

Flowing water seems to be capable of hypnotizing us, of putting us into an altered state of consciousness, when we gaze into it for a spell. The results seem to be consistently positive.

Assuming you have the time and inclination, sit in a comfortable spot, allow your eyes to be drawn into the water, and rest them there. Try for the moment to let go of whatever responsibilities, goals, and expectations the day holds for you. Release any need you have to control outcomes, and see where the water and your mind take you. Perhaps you'll simply rest and unwind, which is hardly an undesirable result. Maybe you'll be totally lost in your thoughts for a time. Maybe it'll become a peaceful meditation. Maybe you'll somehow find yourself sharing communion with the watery depths of nature and with the ubiquitous flow of life, or get a glimpse of the core of your own being.

If you're feeling fatigued or lazy, any explorations, discoveries, or meditations can always wait for another day. You could simply rest and "do nothing," which is a choice many of us make too infrequently in or out of nature. If you're tired, try letting yourself doze off and sleep a bit by the water. There are few better places in the world for a nap than alongside a slow-moving stream or a rushing river, although those of us who are inexperienced won't always feel safe and comfortable enough to indulge ourselves in such an environment. Sleep here, however, will often be unusually deep, restful, and satisfying. Select an inviting spot in the grass, on a bed of moss, or on a big flat or sloping rock. Whether you nap or not, don't be surprised if you start to feel glued there and find it difficult to tear yourself away later on.

Waterfalls and Cascades

No matter how often we visit waterfalls they never lose their power or pull on us. It's not just the scenic prospect they present, including the riveting appeal of watching water tumble from the heights into a natural pool with a thundering roar and an explosion of spray before continuing its journey downstream. The air feels charged around a waterfall, which is perhaps because of all the negative ions, and the rushing water can be utterly mesmerizing. It's common to experience a heightened sense of well-being there.

Waterfalls that are close to roads understandably tend to attract crowds. For the purposes of communing with nature it's worth getting well off the beaten path to find lightly visited falls, though this may mean following a rugged hiking trail or an unmarked path for some distance. There's no better destination to have as part of a nature walk or hike than a waterfall, which is guaranteed to make a lovely lunch spot. It's also an ideal place to engage in extended meditation, deep thought, soul-searching, and "talking to nature."

Along many waterways are also cascades, which are basically mini-waterfalls, as well as rapids, where the water dashes, splatters, and sometimes roars over rocks, providing the visitor with an experience not unlike being at a waterfall. Cascades and rapids are most common in mountainous and other regions where it's rocky and the terrain is uneven, where flowing water meets with frequent obstacles as well as drop-offs. Just as with waterfalls, you can often detect and track down cascades and rapids from a distance because they're the noisiest places along a waterway. When the water's high, their roar may drown out conversation. Cascades as well as waterfalls are potentially dangerous to anyone foolish enough to try swimming near or in them when the water is surging. In other than low-water conditions it's best to stay out of the water altogether, since a strong current can easily overpower a person and sweep him or her away.

Communing with a Waterfall

Many guidebooks will tell you where the waterfalls are, and trail maps frequently indicate them with a symbol. You can also ask at a park information center. Remember that the highest and most famous ones may be mobbed with people, especially on weekends, so do a bit of investigating to uncover the least-known and least-accessible falls. Or go on a weekday, off-season, or in inclement weather. If you're not experienced in off-trail travel, visit a waterfall you can get to via a well-marked trail.

When you arrive, let your instincts tell you what to do. Once you see the falling water you may find it difficult to avert your eyes. Staring is certainly permitted. So is spacing out, as long as you're in a safe spot and not at the edge of a drop-off. Before sitting down, you have the option of first exploring the area; if there's a safe and not-too-strenuous trail leading to the top—or heading below, if you've arrived above the falls—you could also check out the view and perspective from there. When feasible, it's worth spending time both above and below.

Sit down on a slab of rock or any other reasonably comfortable place that calls out to you near or across from the water. Let your senses, thoughts, feelings, and consciousness be drawn in and become immersed in the flying, splashing, perpetually moving water. If the waterfall is large and full, you may sense a powerful presence there. Soon the sound may seem to penetrate your entire body and every element of your being. Sometimes you'll notice your skin start to tingle or other sensations from within. Although all kinds of feelings arise in such settings, which can sometimes include negative emotions regarding past events in our lives, be prepared for the possibility that you'll feel uncommonly serene or blissful. You may also find yourself wanting to sleep, which is a need that's worth indulging.

Stay there as long as you like and circumstances permit. You'll need to shift your body periodically, especially if you're sitting or lying on a rock, but it's easy to lose all track of time in such a place. Hours can pass almost without notice. Thus it's wise to have a watch along, especially if you're there in the afternoon and have some distance to walk out. Be sure to leave with time to spare so you don't get caught in the dark. Back at home, notice any sensory reverberations that linger from the experience. Waterfalls have a way of continuing to echo within us for hours or even days after we experience them.

Lakes and Ponds

Equally irresistible to most of us are lakes, ponds, and other natural bodies of water, which tend to be reservoirs of aquatic life and focal points for a wide range of local wildlife and bird life. We're drawn to the large expanses of water, the scenic settings, and the lush vegetation that often surrounds them. Lakes usually are highlights of any natural area, and they serve as wonderful locations for communing with the watery wild.

Standing bodies of water don't announce themselves from a distance in the noisy and irrepressible way that some rivers and streams do, except on windy days when waves may break and noisily pound the shores. More often, especially at smaller lakes and ponds, the water makes soft sounds as it lightly laps at the sandy or rocky shores, sometimes joined by tree-stirring breezes. Few ways of being "unoccupied" are lovelier than sitting and gazing out at some open blue water, watching approaching waves rise and fall, birds circle and swoop down to catch fish, and shape-shifting clouds drift slowly by.

In warmer weather the water beckons us to enter it as well, although fear, unfamiliarity, or other inclinations will sometimes cause us to refrain. Slipping into pristine waters provides a range of physical and sensuous delights, including the cooling refreshment that's always welcome in summer, as well as vigorous exercise if we choose to swim any distance. Going in allows us to experience bodily communion with the water. In a short time we're likely to notice our skin tingling, our senses stimulated, and more often than not, our spirits soaring.

Circumnavigating a Lake

Some natural lakes and ponds are difficult to approach because they're ringed by thickets of vegetation or wet, marshy areas. Frequently, however, there will be a path or trail leading to a shoreline clearing, which is an appealing place to park your body for a while. If you want to explore the area, try making a circuit of the lake. This is easiest to do if there's a clear, well-marked trail to follow around it. You can also make your own path if you feel a bit adventurous and the ground isn't too wet or the foliage too dense. There's no way to get lost as long as you stay in sight of the water, and you can turn around anytime the going gets too difficult.

Begin by following the most open path, if there is one, that runs reasonably close to the shore. Sometimes you'll be able to walk right alongside the water, especially if there's a beach. Often there'll be many inlets or small bays, meaning your route may be extremely winding and circuitous. Notice the kinds of trees and plants growing near the water and how they differ from those farther inland. Watch for wildlife that may be approaching the lake from any direction to drink, cool off, clean themselves in the water, or search for food. Upon sighting any animal, stay completely still to reduce your chances of being detected or of scaring them away.

Notice how your eyes keep returning to the water no matter what else enters your visual field. Stop anywhere you like— and as often as you like—to look directly out at the lake. Are there waterbirds feeding, squawking, floating, swimming, or diving? Can you spot any fish or other creatures in the water? Watch the waves, ripples, and other patterns. Or on a windless day, gaze across the glassy, mirrorlike, sky-reflecting surface; aim at achieving a similar quietness and equanimity in your mind. If it's a large lake with many bays, allow plenty of extra time to make a complete circuit. When you include possible detours around inlets and other obstacles, the actual distance you'll walk to get around a lake or pond may be several times that of its diameter. If the season and weather are right, consider adding spice to your day with a swim.

The Ocean

Millions of people brave summer crowds to swim and sun themselves at the shore. While thousands of attractive inland lakes are developed for public recreation, the most impressive beaches and shorelines tend to be found oceanside, along our coastal states. The beaches and adjacent lands are frequently overdeveloped, but people come for the sand, surf, and seemingly endless expanses of open water. The best time for communing with the sea from such vantage points is off-season, when few sunworshipers will be found and seabirds have the run of the place.

There are also a limited number of wilder, less accessible beaches on some public lands, which require a hike of a few miles or more to reach. These are well worth seeking out for the quiet solitude and ecological diversity, including scores of wild species you'll never find at a public beach. Here, without the possible summer distractions of radios, picnicking, and partying, you can relate to the ocean uninterrupted and unhindered.

Opening Yourself to the Sea

It's easy to make a meditation out of watching the waves roll in from the sea, and it's helpful to sit quietly and comfortably facing the water for a time with an attitude of receptivity and openness. On the other hand, the ocean will probably work its wonders on you no matter what you do. If you prefer to be more active, take a walk along the beach near the water. Let the sounds of the waves break gently over you, stirring and soothing you, and filling, refreshing, and then emptying your mind. With the ebbing of each wave, imagine that the water is washing away your worries and carrying them out to sea.

You'll probably find your nervous system becoming entrained with the surf's rhythmic, watery ballet, which is extremely relaxing and restorative to a weary brain, jangled nerves, or a sense of disconnection. See if you can notice the sounds of the pounding surf starting to resonate deeply within you; sometimes they'll unearth buried feelings. Imagine that you hear and feel the heartbeat or the in-and-out breath of the ocean itself, as if you're at the feet of (and honoring, drawing support from, and gaining energy from) a giant, ancient grandparent.

The ocean is one of those places you're unlikely to ever forget or get completely out of your system. You'll probably recall it vividly even years later, so strong is the impression a great body of water makes on one's being and senses. Return to the ocean whenever you can. If you live far inland, however, a natural lake can be a suitable substitute and offers some of the same healing properties.

Snow and Ice

Water crystallizes as it freezes, and when this happens in clouds the result is often falling snow, which coats the earth during winter in colder climates—beautifully capturing and holding the precipitation that usually disappears into the ground during the warmer months. With snow and ice the waters of life are especially brightly and beautifully displayed, and they remain visible as long as the temperatures remain below freezing, which is also the very time when many life-forms are dormant or have otherwise sought shelter. Chapter 19 will return to the subject of snow and also discuss the other elements of weather.

You need to bundle up to enjoy snow and ice, but they can be wonderful objects of study, meditation, and contemplation, from individual snowflakes and ice crystals to the entire snow-covered landscape, including gorgeously sculpted snowdrifts, icicles, and ice formations. On a sunny day, these can be so dazzling as to be almost blinding. You can also walk in it, snowshoe in it, ski in it, and play in it. With enough protection—preferably including waterproof pants or something waterproof under you—you can even sit in it for a while.

While resting and thinking about this delightfully strange substance, which is made from the very same element we meet in so many other contexts, we can watch and feel the snow melt right out from under us because of the weight and warmth of our bodies and sometimes also from the heat of the sun. On a warm day in winter or early spring, we'll see little trickles and puddles of water form in the snow and move at gravity's behest toward the nearest stream. Thus water is forever recycling itself throughout the seasons, throughout the external environments of the earth, and throughout the life process itself, including via the tissues and chambers of our own bodies and those of other living things.

15

⁓⊗⁓

BEFRIENDING THE FLORA

AN ENDLESS VARIETY, richness, and abundance of flora and fauna are found throughout the natural world. Only in human-centered environments is this extraordinary diversity of life severely restricted. The majority of us now live in a kind of biological desert from which the bulk of creation has been banished. This is another reason why we need to exit often from civilization to roam the gardens of nature.

Most of us are personally familiar with a relatively small number of other species, in marked contrast with our hunter-gatherer ancestors who knew hundreds or thousands of living things. Our own circle of acquaintances among other species tends to be limited to the common flora and fauna of our region, plus any plants or foods we may grow, and also our pets. Since our culture doesn't encourage us to get to know our natural neighbors, there are countless other species we fail to notice and know little about, even though they may live practically under our noses.

How far each of us goes to befriend other beings is up to us, but we clearly benefit from breaking out of the "human clique" and broadening our interspecies knowledge and contacts. The wider the range of relationships we cultivate among other living things, the stronger will be our sense of membership in the entire earth community and probably the deeper our feelings of affinity with all of life.

An especially wide evolutionary divide lies between ourselves and our floral relatives, yet most of us have little difficulty crossing it mentally or emotionally. We come to love or appreciate scores of plant species—some because they're among our favorite foods and others because of their flowering beauty and delectable fragrances. They're so different from us and at the same time so attractive or distinctive. Even the ones we find unappealing or noxious usually prove to have interesting qualities if we're willing to look more closely. It can be inspiring to witness such amazing manifestations of life.

Trees

If the plant world has wise elders it would have to be the trees, which are capable of living hundreds of years or more—standing so tall and firm with roots that often run deep into the earth, and yet with upper bodies and branches that bend with the wind. During the warmer months, most trees are cloaked in a leafy green elegance and beauty. When denuded in winter, they present a much starker but still imposing appearance against the sky. Some giants, like redwoods and sequoias, are absolutely stunning and humbling to behold; their ancient groves form natural cathedrals.

These incredibly solid and stately living things are ordinarily destined to outlive us at least several times over. Huge trees covered much of this country before the Europeans arrived, but most of our forests today are young because of repeated cutting. In modern times tree mortality has continued to rise, due in part to the harmful effects of air pollution, acid rain, blights, parasites, global warming, and severe storms that have been increasing in the wake of a warmer atmosphere. Especially destructive for trees has been the massive amount of unsustainable logging taking place around the planet, including in our own country, with old-growth trees among the most unfortunate targets.

Without trees the earth's environment and our own health would be in a sorry state at best, given how much of the oxygen we need they produce and how much of the carbon dioxide that we and our industrial civilization have been creating without restraint they absorb. Many species of animals and birds also depend on trees for their living quarters. We should never take trees for granted; they need all the help they can get. It's our responsibility to see that local forests are well protected and to encourage our leaders to provide public funding to plant many more trees.

Take a tree tour around your yard, neighborhood, and the nearest park. If you don't already know their names, bring a tree field guide to help you distinguish between species. Get to know a few individuals really well, paying at least a brief daily visit to one or more trees. Perhaps you could do this on your way to and from work each day. Make note of all the changes you observe through the passing seasons.

Getting in Touch with a Tree

Approach a tree that you want to befriend, get to know, or study. Touching is not only allowed but strongly recommended. Carefully stroke and feel the bark with your hands and observe the texture, which can vary from smooth or slick to rough and craggy. Avoid any vines encircling the tree that might be poison ivy. Look for holes that insects or woodpeckers may have made. Are there cavities large enough to house a bird or small animal? Can you spot any nests perched in the branches above? Keep an eye out for other possible residents like chipmunks and squirrels, who will sometimes scurry about in the canopy of leaves and branches, and who will use the tree trunk as a vertical thoroughfare when you're not there. Take a close look at the leaves or needles and note the size, shape, and other characteristics that will help you identify the tree. Investigate any flowers or fruit as well.

Try stretching your arms around the tree trunk. As you probably know, people who want to protect wild areas and defend endangered species are sometimes called "tree huggers," which doesn't have to be taken as an objectionable epithet. Whether or not you want to hug or be in other physical or emotional contact with a tree is entirely your own business. The worst that could probably happen if you regularly hug trees is an occasional uncomprehending passerby may conclude you're a bit strange. You might also find that it's surprisingly satisfying to express affection and appreciation to a tree, which by no means requires you to neglect or in any way renounce your relationships with people.

While touching the tree, see if you can sense any of the life energy that flows within the trunk, through the branches, and out into the leaves. As long as the tree is alive, a carbon dioxide–breathing being indeed exists behind the sometimes thick and seemingly impenetrable bark. During the warmer seasons some truly incredible processes take place within trees and other green plants, including the sun-assisted manufacturing of food via photosynthesis.

If you spend some time getting to know a tree, it becomes impossible to see it as a mere object or as "potential board feet of lumber," which is how our economy prefers to view trees. Those accustomed to objectifying living things probably consider relating to trees in a personal way to be silly or preposterous. Yet it's precisely such unfeeling attitudes that make possible the current massive undermining of our ecosystem.

Acknowledge any feelings you may have regarding the tree. Is there anything unexpected about your response to it? Would it be a stretch to imagine relating to this or any other tree in the way you might to a person, pet, or something else you care about? You're by no means required to do so, and it's OK if you're unaware of having any particular emotional connection or reaction to trees. However, it's also clearly therapeutic for us to talk and relate to other living things, which is why some people talk to their plants. Claims are made, in fact, that flora respond to being talked to by growing faster and becoming healthier. Whether or not that's true, there's little doubt that we feel better when we attempt to communicate or commune with trees and other plants, a practice that apparently was normal behavior for our earth-dwelling ancestors. What might you say to a tree? Try it, if you dare, with different trees and see what happens.

These days it's much more common for people to touch trees in much less direct and personal ways, such as by using them as backrests, a practice that surely goes back tens of millennia or further. Sitting or standing with your spine against the tree trunk is indeed a great way to center and ground yourself. In that position you'll sometimes find stress discharging almost of its own accord. There are few better sites for resting, reading, pondering important problems, and meditating.

Other Plants

Trees are merely the oldest, largest, and most majestic members of the plant world. Thousands of other flora fill every possible niche of the natural world—bushes, shrubs, vines, ferns, herbs, grasses, seaweed, mosses, lichen, and many other kinds of plants. Some are colorful and eye-catching; others have unassuming appearances and blend in with the landscape, thus requiring attentiveness and skill to locate and identify them. Many species disappear entirely from view during winter and then quietly reemerge in spring. Yet every variety of flora seems to have a place or a role to play in the natural community.

Among the plants we know relatively little about, think of the hundreds or thousands of herbs that have healthful medicinal properties. Many of these were used by our ancestors and still play important roles in some traditional cultures, whereas in the Western world we've only begun to relearn what's important about these forgotten species. Or how about all the edible plants we're equally ignorant of? An enormous bounty of flora grows in the natural world that we could use for food (although we do have an obligation to refrain from picking them in protected areas). Other than recognizable fruits like blueberries or strawberries, however, most of us know very few wild edibles.

Getting to know nature well requires surveying and examining the widest possible selection of wild plants and other floral beings, including the "little guys." It's necessary to get on our hands and knees—or at least to scour the ground with our eyes—to spot some of the smaller flora, which may be hidden in the shadows or obscured by bushes or tall grasses. No matter how familiar we are with an area and its residents, in poking around we'll usually come face-to-face with fascinating strangers who have previously eluded our detection.

Appreciating a Plant

Each time you go out into nature, make it your business to become acquainted with a plant you're relatively unfamiliar with. If you're engaged in recreational activities, do this when you're taking a break. Sit down as close as you can to the plant of your choice, preferably without crushing or trampling its neighbors. This may be impossible in an area dense with vegetation, but do your best to tread lightly.

Carefully touch and examine the plant. You should already know how to recognize poison ivy, poison oak, and poison sumac, which can be learned from a plant identification book; you'll want to avoid inadvertently coming into contact with one of these "less friendly" plants, which produce an extremely itchy and unpleasant rash in many of us. Watch out as well for the sharp thorns or spines that protect some bushes and other plants, for stinging nettles that cause an intense itch, and also for small animals or biting or stinging insects that could be hiding beneath the leaves.

Study the plant's observable characteristics. If it's new to you, a plant book can help you identify it and give you some additional information. Spending time attending to this and other species in person should leave the flora embedded in your mind and memory, meaning you're almost certain to recognize it the next time you see it. How many "siblings" does the plant seem to have in the immediate area? And throughout the greater region? Does it appear to be an abundant species here or a rarity?

Try reflecting or meditating on this particular rooted being that you're getting to know. Does the plant communicate, convey, or suggest anything to you? How interested in it are you? No need to apologize if you can't work up enthusiasm for one or more of your most distant relatives; on the other hand, you might note a remarkable feeling of affinity and warmth on your part, which should similarly not be grounds for embarrassment. How might its life intersect with those of other species? Are there signs that insects or animals have nibbled on its leaves? How much, if at all, might one plant—or for that matter, any other single being, including a person—make a difference in this world?

On each outing choose a different kind of vegetation to get closer to. Seek the widest possible range of species, perhaps sitting with a fern one time, a large bush the next, and a patch of moss the following time. Before long, everywhere you go in nature you'll find floral acquaintances and friends, and your sense of comfort and belonging should continually increase. When you can relate to other species, your experiences in nature are almost certain to be more interesting and fulfilling than if you walk through the natural world as an uninvolved onlooker or use nature to de-stress without really noticing who's there.

Flowers

Few elements of nature are capable of capturing our attention more effectively than flowers, which have long had special emotional and spiritual meaning for human beings. Thus they're always included in our most important life rituals, ceremonies, and celebrations. They're also universally given as an expression of love and respect. Flowers seem to signify for us the eternal blossoming of life itself.

Many plants flower for a time each year that's all too short for most of us. The primary purpose of the bright colors and irresistible scents is naturally to attract bees and other insects, which assist in pollination and plant reproduction. Yet it's easy to imagine that the astonishing beauty and seductive fragrances of flowers might have been fashioned to meet our needs alone. Picturing a flowerless world, which would be painfully plain and drab, is extremely difficult for us. And it's almost impossible to see them solely as accidents of evolution.

Flowering plants continually intrude into our consciousness when we explore nature in springtime and early summer, and to a lesser extent throughout the rest of the growing season. When we're not in a hurry and don't have other things to do, it's tempting to stop and marvel—no matter how familiar we are with a particular species—especially when they're just starting to bloom. Some flowers are so tiny that they're easy to miss unless we're on the lookout for them. Others utterly dominate or overwhelm the landscape when they're blossoming—as, for example, when stands of mountain laurel or rhododendron come into flower each year, leaving the air heavy with perfume and entire hillsides or mountainsides painted white, pink, or purple.

Getting Familiar with Flowers

Turn on your flower-detector whenever you enter the natural world during spring and summer—which requires keeping your eyes as well as your nostrils wide open. Try taking a slow and deliberate flower walk when you're up for a leisurely outing, wherein you pause or stop to investigate whatever blossoms you encounter. When a common species is in bloom, you probably won't be able to miss them as blankets of flowers may be everywhere. After you've luxuriated in them, however, direct your antennae elsewhere to detect their less conspicuous neighbors. Finding flowers is rarely difficult or frustrating since the bright colors usually stand out vividly, especially against a backdrop of green vegetation.

Spend a little time with each variety of flower, standing or sitting as close as you can. Allow your vision to go into soft focus, and let the stunning colors and sensual shapes fill and feed your eyes. Some of the amazing qualities of the natural world can deeply stir us and inspire wonder if we merely relax and let go of any preconceptions. One of the many places to rediscover awe is amid the achingly rich beauty of newly opened blossoms. Savor the fragrances as well; while some will be subdued, others are impossibly sweet and intoxicating.

During the blooming season make an effort at least once a week to visit the woods, meadows, or desert in search of wild-flowers. Their limited life spans and often small sizes will make the less abundant species a challenge to locate. You're almost guaranteed to discover different flowers and a somewhat new scene each week. Even if you know an area intimately, you can never predict exactly what you'll find at any particular time since rainfall, temperature, and other environmental factors vary from one week to the next. Also, there's constant competition taking place among species. Remember that picking flowers or vegetation is illegal in many parks and preserves. Where it's allowed, take only those that are extremely abundant and leave the rest alone.

Mushrooms, Mosses, and Other Life-Forms

Nature is replete with smaller plants and other organisms that can easily escape our notice, yet many are well worth looking for. Among those of special interest to us are mushrooms, since the edible varieties make a delicious contribution to our diet. These fungi tend to spring up overnight after rainfall. As we all should know, because of the potential danger from poisonous varieties only experts at mushroom identification should forage for wild mushrooms and eat what they collect.

We're drawn to mosses for quite different reasons. During seasons of adequate rainfall, they're soft, moist, and lush little plants that tend to form a thick, irresistibly green carpet on undisturbed rocks, fallen trees, and occasionally, the forest floor. They invite our touch; however, mosses are easily torn by our footwear, so we should try to avoid walking on them. Also sometimes covering rocks where moisture is prevalent are lichen, the often colorful symbiotic combination of algae and fungi.

These members of the floral world are merely a few of the better-known representatives of a much larger community. If you choose to explore the natural plant world at some length, you'll encounter and become acquainted with a much more vast array of living things. No matter how much time you choose to spend there, you'll never come even remotely close to exhausting the possibilities. Life in the natural world is too varied and complex for us to ever completely uncover or know; there's always something interesting around the bend awaiting our discovery.

16

❦

TRACKING THE FAUNA

MOST OF US are curious about wildlife, especially our mammalian relatives, although some of us may be a bit uneasy about the possibility of actually coming face-to-face with them in the wild. Contrary to the impression given by many TV nature shows, however, the odds that we'll encounter wildlife at close quarters are quite slim. Most wild animals prefer to keep their distance from us and succeed in doing so.

The occasional sighting or meeting with a large mammal is usually a thrilling surprise. While there are locations in the natural world where we're more likely to see wildlife, it's difficult to predict where they'll be and when; thus we're frequently caught off-guard. If we go photo-hunting for such animals as bear or moose, we can't expect them to appear on cue, and we'll usually be disappointed if we want them to pose for us. If they show up at all, they seem to have a knack of doing so when our camera is packed away and we're preoccupied with other things.

Although some animals like moose or porcupine look a little strange to us, most creatures are truly beautiful beings, and some move around with amazing grace. Our eyes can't help but be riveted on them on the rare occasions when they're nearby. What's both scary and inspiring about meeting wildlife is experiencing in person their unrestricted freedom and impressive physical agility and power—which may make us aware of our vulnerability since they can behave as they please in our presence. Obviously most wild animals could seriously harm us if they wanted to; but as long as we don't threaten them or invade their space, they'll usually show us similar respect.

Locating Wildlife

Getting to know wildlife well on their home turf is a special challenge—and it's a great deal more difficult than communing with the plant world. We need considerable skill if we want to actively search for and find the majority of wild animal species and get close enough to observe them. After all, most creatures can smell us, hear us, and take evasive action long before we have any hint of their whereabouts. Inexperienced visitors sometimes have the impression that the woods are almost devoid of wild animals. It's true that larger mammals were hunted out some time ago and are therefore absent from some natural areas, but even where well-represented, most are good at steering clear of us.

On the other hand, some creatures are much less shy about our presence than others, and as long as we keep a safe distance they may continue to go about their business as we wander by. Even with the most elusive animals there's always the slight possiblity of a chance meeting. If we spend enough time in the natural world, our paths are bound to cross those of a wide range of wild species. Occasionally an animal will inadvertently walk right in front of us, having somehow failed to see, hear, or smell us. This happens most often when we've been sitting quietly and the animal is upwind from us. In such unexpected encounters we usually have only a couple of seconds before they're gone. If we're close enough, however, some animals will momentarily freeze from fear. Others will pause to assess the danger or perhaps satisfy their curiosity about us before fleeing. They may await our first move, and if we remain motionless the interspecies meeting could continue for up to several minutes or more.

Easiest to locate are the more ubiquitous smaller mammals like squirrels and chipmunks, which inhabit urban and suburban areas as well as wilder places. Also commonly seen are the ever-abundant deer that frequent wooded areas. How animals behave around human beings can vary enormously depending on where we encounter them. Those that have been fed and are used to people may come right up to you in search of a handout, whereas in the wild the same species may not let you get anywhere near them.

If wildlife viewing or photography is your avocation and priority, it's helpful to cultivate patience and perseverance. You might have to wait hours or days or take a number of trips before a particular species puts in an appearance. You can increase your chances by learning more about the animal and where it's most likely to be found. Park rangers can contribute tips about where to look. Constant vigilance is called for, though you may also want to bring a book along for the waiting process. To maximize your chances of a sighting, stay as quiet and still as possible. Talking with friends or moving around will effectively announce your presence to all wildlife in the area. It's best to lean or sit against a tree, in some bushes, or in tall grass where your body won't stand out from the background. Wear clothing of muted natural colors that blend in with your surroundings.

Since a number of creatures are nocturnal, you won't find a full representation of the wildlife population if you limit your ventures to daylight hours alone. Two of the best times for wildlife-viewing are around sunrise and sunset, when more animals are usually on the move. At these times you have the greatest chance of catching sight of some nocturnal species you're unlikely to otherwise see.

Meeting and observing wildlife is typically a treat, but it's important to know how to behave in their presence. For safety's sake, always keep your distance from any wild animal you encounter, no matter how innocent and nonaggressive it might appear. Even the smallest creature can attack or bite if it feels threatened or cornered, and you may have little time to defend yourself. Be especially cautious in the presence of larger mammals like bear, elk, or bison, which should never be approached under any circumstance. Upon sighting such an animal, stand quietly, observe, and perhaps take your photo, but never ever try to get closer or advance on it. If the animal makes sounds or shows other possible signs of aggression or alarm, back off slowly while facing it and avert your eyes to the side to show deference. If you fail to respect its space, you're at risk of being charged. Attacks are extremely rare, however, and the odds are greatly in your favor as long as you exercise caution and restraint. Most animals will retreat or run the other way before you have a chance to do anything.

Watching Wildlife

When you run, hike, or walk fast through a natural area, you're likely to see little in the way of wildlife. Your movements and the noise of your footsteps will tip off the entire creature community to your passing, although there's always a chance that you'll have an occasional brief encounter with an animal that's similarly on the move. To see the most wildlife, you need to stop and stay put for a while, preferably in a place that offers at least limited shelter or protection so you can't be easily spotted, such as amid boulders, trees, bushes, or other dense vegetation. If you want to move, try a slow, silent walk. Strive to make an absolute minimum of noise in the process; this can be challenging to accomplish on a crunchy forest floor.

When an animal appears or you spy one in the distance, stay absolutely still. If you're lucky you may have gone unnoticed; some animals have relatively poor vision and find it difficult to detect and identify others that aren't moving, especially when the latter can't be smelled because the wind is absent or blowing the wrong way. Sometimes even when they're aware of you, they'll stick around to investigate out of curiosity, although the slightest movement on your part may send them racing away.

What you'll see and experience with wildlife is never entirely predictable, which is what makes it scary to some of us and exciting to many others. Sighting and coming in contact with wild animals is frequently a moving and inspiring prospect.

Sometimes their behavior seems remarkably human or at least familiar and understandable, and so we find our empathy stirred. At other times we may sense we're looking at lovely but incomprehensible beings who live on the far side of a great evolutionary gulf. One of the qualities that stands out is the vibrant energy and aliveness many wild creatures display when seen close up. Their domesticated relatives tend to appear passive and depressed in comparison.

You shouldn't expect a wild animal to respond to any attempts you may make to communicate with it, but then again, you never know. It can't hurt to carefully and gently reach out to a creature verbally, if you feel so inclined, from a safe distance. Animals are more bound by instinct than we are, but they also exhibit enormous sensory awareness and individuality. Many accounts exist of wild creatures interacting with human beings and intervening when people are in trouble. How much of this is myth and how much reality is unclear. Animal behavior has been inadequately studied in the wild, in part because it's so difficult to observe free-roaming fauna. We do know that our society routinely underestimates animals. It certainly makes sense for us to be as open-minded and respectful as we can toward them.

Tracking Animals

Locating animal tracks is almost always much simpler than spotting the animals who make them, and it's easiest by far in winter. Some elusive species like mountain lions and bobcats are rarely glimpsed by anyone, not even by those who live full-time in their territory, but their tracks turn up fairly regularly. Animal tracks of all kinds are visible in the snow. During the warmer months, the prints are noticeable on muddy trails and roads, although a well-trained eye can find tracks and other signs almost anywhere in the wild.

The ancient art of animal tracking originated with our hunter-gatherer ancestors, and these skills are still known and used by some of the earth's remaining indigenous peoples. Now they're accessible to us as well at schools that teach tracking and wilderness survival skills. With sufficient study and practice, some people can learn to perceive the faintest, most subtle traces of an animal's presence or passage. In addition to footprints, all wildlife leave behind scat (feces), from which we can learn about their diets, as well as other visible signs such as diggings and scratch marks on trees. Tracking skills have long assisted hunters in their pursuit of animals for food, and today these skills are useful as well for wildlife observation, photography, and learning more about animal behavior.

Following a Track

You can look for tracks, scat, and other animal signs at any time of year, but one of the best times to get started is winter, when you'll often find clear tracks in the snow right outside your door and throughout the natural world. Field guides are available to help you identify tracks and scat; taking a course is helpful as well, especially for meeting the challenges of finding tracks during warmer months.

Following tracks in the snow makes for a real winter adventure. If the snow's deep, you'll need snowshoes to get far without exhausting yourself. There's no telling where the tracks could take you. The size and shape of prints and the distance between them give you some information or clues as to the animal's identity. Depending on the snow's consistency, prints may be sharply defined or indistinct. Easiest to track are large mammals, who can't squeeze through tight spaces or leap from ledge to ledge, so you're less likely to lose their trail. In contrast, when following the tracks of a small, agile animal, you may sometimes find yourself stopped and stymied by barriers or hazards like impenetrable thickets of vegetation, steep rock walls, or frozen ponds or waterways that are too thin for you to safely cross.

Be aware of the risk of getting lost whenever you venture well into the wild. The most sensible way to return is to follow your own tracks back to where you started. There's always the risk, however, that some fresh snow or gusty winds could obscure your path and leave you disoriented. It's always wise to carry a compass and a map or to stay within sight of a road or some landform that you can use for orientation. And don't go far without lots of warm clothing, some food, and appropriate safety items.

If the tracks you're following are fresh and you happen to catch sight of the animal, stop immediately. Remain still and don't give in to any temptation to get closer, both for reasons of your own safety and to avoid frightening the animal. Winter is already a difficult time for many fauna, and food is scarce, so you shouldn't add to their stress and fatigue by giving them cause to feel pursued and in danger.

Tracks tell tales throughout the year, including in the warmer, dryer months when it's more difficult to read them. Frequently you'll be following an animal's journey in search of food, and what happened along the way will often be expressed by their paw prints or hoofprints and other marks in the snow, mud, or sand. An animal's itinerary may seem to wind aimlessly, or instead it may head directly for a particular destination, perhaps where food was earlier buried. Evasive actions may have been taken by the animal to avoid becoming food for predators; sometimes you'll find signs of a struggle for life.

Try getting on your hands and knees to put yourself in the physical space of the creature whose tracks you're following. Though there's no way to access their emotional and other inner life, you may nevertheless gain some insights into their existence. Many possible surmises can be made based on the record traced in the snow or soil. You can test some of your conjectures by reading and learning more about wild animal behavior, habits, and food preferences.

Birds

You can learn a lot from the birds in your backyard, but locating and observing birds in the wild is always especially enjoyable and worthwhile. Birding is one of the most popular of all outdoor hobbies and low-key recreational activities. Millions of people head out into nature on a regular basis with their binoculars. As with your efforts to track down and watch other wildlife, you'll see the most by being the quietest and moving the least. The more you can blend in with the scenery, the likelier it is that birds will fly close by, perch in nearby branches, and sometimes land practically in your lap before noticing you're there. If you offer them food they may eventually learn to trust you and, in time, actually land on your shoulders or raised hands.

The natural world would be sadly lacking without the gorgeous colors, soaring flight, and lilting songs of the winged ones, who continuously invite our curiosity and interest with their lively presence. Birders often take pleasure in identifying as many species as possible, but it's also rewarding to simply relax and watch the show as these busy, colorful characters carry on with their daily activities—including snatching insects from the air, chasing intruders out of their territory, building nests, and feeding the young. Binoculars help greatly in keeping close track of them, but quite a bit can be seen with the naked eye— especially in open areas like meadows and from cliff tops, where raptors are frequently observed riding the breezes.

Listening to and being serenaded by birdsong is one of the sublime pleasures of spending time in nature. Particularly in spring and early summer, the woodlands continuously echo with the spirited and sometimes plaintive cries and songs of myriad bird species. If we choose to camp out, we can expect to be awakened in the predawn hours by an increasingly high-volume festival of avian music—a chaotic but inspiring melodic competition.

Birds also impress us with their graceful flight: sometimes taking off in a flash, darting about madly, soaring, swooping, and then landing with instantaneous precision on anything they choose, including the most precarious branches and rocks. Clumsy they are not. And while many species of birds don't advertise themselves, the feather coats of some include the brightest and most strikingly beautiful shades of color found anywhere in the natural world.

Many books and magazines teach the basics and extol the virtues of bird-watching. Beyond identifying species and observing their "antics," take some time to reflect on how life expresses itself through these ancient forms of being we know of as birds, which are said to be more closely related to the dinosaurs than to us. To what extent can you identify with them? Is it possible to vicariously share their flight? Are there lessons about life to be learned from these winged beings?

Populations of some songbirds and other species are unfortunately plummeting due to toxins in the environment and the destruction of their habitats. Like so many other forms of fauna and flora, birds have never been more in need of our assistance. We can take a stand for them by doing everything we can to protect natural areas.

Fish, Amphibians, and Reptiles

It's only natural that we tend to be especially mammal-oriented in our wildlife interests. We can't help paying the most attention to our closest relatives, who share certain physical similarities with us and also happen to include the earth's largest creatures. In looking around the natural world, we often miss or ignore "lower" forms of life. Fish are one partial exception, given their importance in our diet and the traditional popularity of fishing in the United States as an easygoing form of outdoor recreation. But we tend to be much more interested in catching and eating them than in trying to understand them or in any way communing with them.

Among the better-known amphibians are frogs, which are visible as well as audible at so many natural ponds, lakes, and waterways. From spring through early summer, most healthy wetlands echo with the raucous and assertive courting sounds of frogs, ranging from high-pitched spring peepers to deep-voiced bullfrogs. Look for them along the shore of any lake or pond you visit during the warmer months. Common as well are toads and salamanders, which similarly tend to frequent cool, moist areas. You'll often find them hopping or slithering around on the ground during and after rain.

Widely seen reptiles include turtles and snakes, which you're almost certain to come across every now and then on your outings. Fear of snakes is extremely common, and there are indeed some poisonous species to watch out for. But most such fears are out of proportion to the actual danger; the risk of being bitten is minimal. Always pay attention to where you're stepping, however, especially when you go through dense vegetation and can't see what's underfoot. Also, never put your bare hands into a crack or hole, nor onto any high rock or ledge where you can't see what's there. Like most other creatures, snakes aren't interested in socializing with you and will slither away when given the opportunity. Since they're cold-blooded like frogs, you'll usually only find them out in warm weather.

Insects

Few if any of us belong to an insect appreciation society. After all, we call them pests and do what we can to eradicate them. Yes, bugs are rampant in the natural world; the numbers of individual species and total populations are mind-boggling. And we're constantly warned that some insects carry diseases, which is true. But most of these creatures are utterly harmless to human beings. They all play a role in the ecosystem, no matter how unappetizing we may find them: they serve as food for birds and other wildlife, pollinate flowers, and some species assist in breaking down organic matter to fertilize the soil.

Many of us want to avoid and ignore insects, which is our prerogative. Yet among the vast number of species are some of the most fascinating creatures on earth. We don't have to feel affection toward them, but it's helpful if we can learn to cultivate at least a minimal amount of appreciation for them. Maintaining an antagonistic attitude toward insects and certain other species increases our feeling of separateness from and discomfort with the natural world. Being less judgmental, intolerant, and irritated about bugs makes it easier for us to come into community with nature.

Of course, we need to protect ourselves against the relatively few species of insects that are inclined to bite or sting us, such as mosquitoes and biting flies, during the seasons when they're around. This means using bug repellent and perhaps avoiding areas where they're prevalent during peak insect seasons. But since they'll always be here as a part of the ecosystem, we need to accept the fact that some bugs will usually be buzzing around during the warmer seasons and that getting an occasional bite is no big deal. With the exception of people who are seriously allergic to bee stings or other bites, the minor discomfort of a few bug bites every now and then is a small price to pay for the endless rewards and benefits nature bestows on us.

Looking for Bugs

Take a bug walk on a warm day and see who or what you can find. Bugs will sometimes come to you, of course, in the way no other wildlife does. Some can sense the moisture from your skin or breath, or detect any scents you may be wearing, such as from soap, shampoo, deodorant, or perfume. If they're after your blood, you may not feel tolerant nor want to watch them hone in on your skin; yet there are things to be learned from observing them.

The vast majority of insects will show little or no interest in you, so you'll have to seek them out. Many will be found near water, in moist areas, and on vegetation. Some will be crawling around in and under decaying leaf litter on the ground. Some are in the soil well underground, and others you'll find in tree bark, and especially in stumps, downed trees, and dead branches. Some are tiny and practically invisible to the naked eye; others are quite large and may even wear bright colors.

Watching ants going about their business is one nice non-taxing way to while away time on a lazy day. Often, you'll observe them carrying away crumbs from your just-eaten lunch, in the process accomplishing some amazing physical feats, such as dragging items that are many times their size across rough terrain to their colony; two to several ants will sometimes share the effort of transporting a larger piece of food.

It's hard to imagine a creature more different from us than an insect. Yet we do occupy the same ecosystem, and each of us has roles to play here on earth, although our niches and endeavors vary enormously. Bugs are much more specialized than "higher" forms of life, and we can't imagine them being conscious in any meaningful way. Yet like us they eat, sleep, and mate. And since they've been here on the planet a great deal longer than us, they have plenty of seniority over us, although we may not be inclined nor are we required to grant them permission to bite us. We need to acknowledge, if we can find it in ourselves to do so, that they have as much of a right to be here as we do.

17

⚮

INTERACTING WITH
DIVERSE HABITATS

THE EARTH HARBORS a host of different ecosystems and biotic communities, each with its own unique features, "personality," and characteristic life-forms. Among these diverse environments are forests, grasslands, meadows, wetlands, deserts, and tundra. Sometimes several distinctive biological communities share a particular locale and exist in close proximity, whereas in more homogeneous areas a single kind of habitat may predominate.

Which flora and fauna occupy which locale isn't a random matter. The climate, amount of rainfall, available groundwater throughout the year, soil acidity, and other variables make an environment more suitable for some life-forms than for others. Within particular communities are webs of connections and interdependencies among individual species, some of which furnish food for others or contribute in other ways, directly or indirectly, to their well-being. These interrelationships help keep the ecosystem in a state of relative balance or homeostasis.

We benefit from getting to know at least one or more habitats or ecosystems thoroughly, and becoming acquainted with as many of the residents as possible. The most obvious choice will be the natural habitat that we live closest to or that's most accessible to us. It's also helpful to familiarize ourselves with life communities that lie farther afield. But it's probably better to have a deeper awareness and understanding of one environment than a superficial acquaintance or knowledge of many. This chapter will survey several of the better-known habitats. Many others also exist, including some environments discussed in other chapters, such as the mountains and the ocean.

Human Habitats

Before taking a look at some common natural habitats, let's briefly consider such human-created environments as cities, suburbs, and farmlands, where nature nevertheless continues to maintain a significant presence. When it's inconvenient for those of us who live in such areas to visit the wilder places, we can often find substantial slices of the natural world hiding out or sometimes in full display nearby. Earlier in this book we discussed urban and suburban parks, where many trees, smaller plants, and a significant range of wildlife can frequently hold their own. Some larger parks have lakes and ponds as well as attractive natural terrain, including hills, cliffs, and rock formations. There are also many public and private gardens to be found in developed areas.

Other places where wild flora and fauna have successfully adapted include vacant city lots; areas along fences, walls, and other property boundaries; and the lands alongside many roads, highways, and railroad tracks. Among these residents are numerous wildflowers; a considerable variety of wild plants; a diverse bird life including geese, ducks, and such species as owl, raven, and vulture; as well as wildlife that can include raccoon, opossum, woodchuck, fox, and coyote.

Forests

There may be no quicker way to leave civilization behind than by entering the great community of trees that comprises a forest, an environment that was home to some of our earliest primate ancestors. Not everyone enjoys the closed-in feeling of a forest, but immersing ourselves in the world of wild, free-growing trees can feel extremely nourishing if we're open to it. Oxygen levels in forests are usually high during the leaf season, which is probably one reason we often experience a sense of heightened well-being there. Other forms of life prosper as well in the fertile forest universe.

The appearance and feel of each particular forest is a function of the species of trees that grow there, along with the other flora and fauna that call the area home, all of which have certain environmental and climatic requirements. A forest of pine, spruce, and other conifers has a completely different feel from one of maple, oak, and other broadleaf species, and an old-growth forest is almost entirely unlike a recently cut woodland that consists mainly of saplings.

Enormous forests of ancient trees once covered much of the earth's surface. While cutting has been accelerating and trees are rapidly disappearing in many places around the planet, huge expanses of forest fortunately remain in our country and in some other lands. The majority of us in the United States don't have to travel far to find a forest; except where desert or grasslands predominate, most public parks include forested areas.

Taking a Forest Walk

Any forest is worth walking in—or resting, recreating, or doing almost anything else under the sun in. Walking is one of the easiest and least intrusive ways to enter a forest, although you may need to drive to get there. Return to the forest of your choice as often as you can, but periodically try to walk in others as well. Attempt to identify what distinguishes one tree community from another, and see if there are differences in how you feel in each. It's all right to play favorites, but respect that each forest and tree has a right to exist for its own sake.

As you walk or hike along, allow the dizzying, never-ending array of trees to greet you as they continuously sweep past on either side, inviting you to venture ever deeper into their community. Note the variability that's observable even within a single species: the range of ages, sizes, and appearances. Don't ignore the fallen trees, downed branches, and rotting stumps, which play important roles in the tree world; the dead and decaying among all life-forms fertilize the soil for the benefit of future generations. You can stop anytime you like to examine individual members of the assembly, but also notice any forest-minded perceptions or insights you have while on the move.

A forest experience will engage most of your senses. An older forest in particular is often a treasure trove of rich, earthy scents; of melodious sounds as well as sharp or startling cries from birds and chattering from chipmunks and squirrels; of creaking, talking trees that sometimes whine ominously in the wind; of a visual tapestry of dark earth colors, especially deep greens and browns, sometimes specked with bright wildflowers; and of a mix of surfaces and textures that range from craggy bark to spongy earth layered with pine needles.

It's easy to see why spending time in a place as life-intensive as a forest feels like such a respite and refuge from the modern world. Older forests often strongly suggest natural hermitages and cathedrals, and the open areas beneath their lofty arching branches frequently have the feel of sacred spaces. Not coincidently, spending time in such a forest seems to facilitate the processes of inner healing, restoration, and spiritual renewal.

Meadows

Whereas visiting a dense forest can be like entering a vast, protective, wooded womb, spending time in a meadow means occupying the most expansive of natural spaces—an unobstructed, airy, exhilarating place where breezes and winds run totally wild and the skies are always completely open to our examination. If it's located on a hillside or mountainside, a meadow is sure to offer an appealing vista as well. Here the setting seems to encourage us to loosen or free our thoughts from confinement or containment. This is a place to discover fresh perspectives on the world, ourselves, nature, and life itself.

It's easy to while away some leisurely hours in a mountain meadow watching hawks circle in search of prey, insects going about their business in the waving grasses, and the distant, ant-sized inhabitants of our own civilization carrying on in the foothills and valleys below. But enclosed, viewless meadows and forest clearings that lie at lower elevations can be inviting as well. All are excellent places to observe the comings and goings of wildlife, especially if we choose to lay low in the grasses to minimize our visibility.

Exploring a Meadow

A meadow is a place to sit and explore at close range, preferably on your hands and knees. Examine the different grasses and small plants, and look for wildflowers. You may also come across some small tree seedlings that are attempting to colonize the area. In the process of exploring you'll probably also meet a selection of insects and perhaps find some concealed holes where snakes or small mammals may live, although you're unlikely to meet the occupants; some of them are nocturnal and sleep underground during the day, and the others use their senses and skills to avoid you. Larger wildlife, including deer or elk, are likely to visit the meadow regularly to dine on its grasses, and birds are sure to frequent it for insect meals.

After you've done a respectable survey of the meadow's stationary inhabitants, while continuing to keep an eye out for any four-footed residents or flying citizens, you've got a few other sedentary choices open to you if you choose to linger. One perennial favorite is to lie back in the grass and indulge in some serious sky- and cloud-watching, or stargazing if you stay past sunset or return at night. Remaining after dark is only advisable if you have a dependable flashlight and are certain you won't get lost.

An open meadow is a perfect place for reflecting on the larger questions, considering your life purpose, pondering problems, finding solutions, setting goals, and envisioning ways of living that better meet your needs and the earth's as well. Soaring birds, drifting clouds, buffeting breezes, and rippling grasses all tend to get the imagination flowing and will often give rise to more expansive and creative ideas. If you fall asleep or deliberately decide to nap, attempt to recall any dreams afterward and notice what's on your mind upon awakening; the content could provide some more food for your ruminations.

Grasslands

Grasslands previously extended across much of the middle of the United States. Significant remnants of these once seemingly endless meadows remain, although in large areas the grasses have long been plowed under by agriculture, which has transformed so much of the landscape into unnaturally neat rows of crops. Prairie lands are especially notable for their extraordinary openness—the grassy earth extending to all horizons and the sky coming all the way down to meet the ground. Here the inverted bowl of the sky dominates both day and night. Nowhere else are storms or the starry night sky more dramatically displayed.

Grasses range from shorter varieties, which predominate in the eastern Rockies, to midwestern tallgrasses that can reach as high as seven or eight feet. Groves of trees, rocky knolls, and winding streams occasionally break the seeming uniformity of grasslands. Cattle and horses are widely allowed to graze in such areas, even on many public lands, although a range of wildlife also usually resides here, including prairie dog, pronghorn, elk, and the once-ubiquitous bison. The openness of grasslands invites human beings to roam, rest, and reflect as well. Like meadows, where grasses thrive on a much smaller scale, we find ourselves feeling uncommonly comfortable here. It's the kind of habitat our primate ancestors apparently inhabited and strongly favored after descending from the trees, which may still be reflected in our preference for (or obsession with) grassy lawns.

Swamps, Marshes, and Other Wetlands

For most people a swamp has more negative than positive connotations and associations. It's easy to picture bug-infested waters, deep muck, and plenty of unsavory creatures like alligators, snakes, and other reptiles. While this reputation isn't entirely unearned, there's a lot about swamps that's fascinating or at least interesting. They also play a valuable role in the larger ecosystem, as do other wetlands—providing essential habitat for waterfowl and many other birds, as well as helping prevent floods in times of excessive rainfall by holding water that might otherwise overflow waterways.

Most swamps aren't easy places to visit on foot, given how much of the land is usually wet or under water. But protected swamps in parks or private sanctuaries often have convenient boardwalks or elevated walkways to allow safe entry into their inner recesses; without such aids we may only be able to wander around a swamp's perimeter. The best way of all to explore a good-size swamp that has discrete waterways or a significant amount of standing water is in a canoe, kayak, or raft. Swamps that freeze in winter become much more accessible on foot, but this is unfortunately the very time of year when much of the vegetation and wildlife are dormant or in hiding.

You're not required to love or even like swamps, but it's interesting to visit one once in a while to see the diverse and sometimes exotic flora and fauna. Some of the great swamps of the South are junglelike with dense foliage, featuring old cypress and other water-tolerant trees. To visit such a place is truly to enter another world. Like deserts, swamps will never win popularity contests, but they nevertheless attract substantial numbers of enthusiasts. Insects may have the potential to disrupt your peace of mind in these environments, so come armed with a good supply of bug repellent. Yet there are times when insects won't be present in annoying numbers; on cool, windy, or rainy days they probably won't bother you at all.

Whereas swamps are often dominated by trees and bushes, marshes are more open and resemble wet meadows, and because of their openness they attract an especially wide variety of waterbirds. During times of migration the visiting bird population changes daily if not hourly, and sometimes a marsh will be absolutely overrun with waterfowl and raucous with their vocalizations. Here, too, you're much better off in a boat than on foot. But you can always walk along the shore of a marsh and perhaps even wade in a bit, which is easiest and most palatable in hip boots. Other wetlands include the streams, rivers, lakes, and ponds discussed in Chapter 14—as well as bogs, which are waterlogged areas of peat and decaying matter, often with vegetation that includes mosses, grasses, and shrubs.

Meandering Around a Swamp or Marsh

Many of us have swamps or marshes within a few miles of where we live, but most of these aren't suitable for foot travel. Find a marsh or swamp in a park or local preserve that has boardwalks or other constructed walkways that will let you see and explore the innards of the swamp. Aside from public parks, a number of Audubon Society sanctuaries, Nature Conservancy preserves, and other private nature centers around the country include wetlands with elevated walkways. Since you may encounter wet or muddy areas along some trails, especially during spring and after rainfall, wear rubber-soled boots or shoes and always bring your bug repellent.

Swamps and marshes are rarely quiet places, except in winter. Listen and enjoy the birdsong, buzzing insects, croaking frogs, and whatever else you can distinguish from the chorus or cacophony. You'll notice that most creatures become silent as you approach, which helps protect them from predators. Look for signs of muskrats and other aquatic mammals, great blue herons and other lovely waterbirds, as well as snakes and other reptiles. See if you can identify scents in the air as well; in late spring or summertime there are usually plenty of them, ranging from pungent and acrid around stagnant waters to wonderfully fragrant in the presence of flowering plants.

Most of us have learned to consider swamps repugnant. To what extent does that fit with your actual experience while exploring one? Notice what interests you and what you find appealing and attractive, as well as what, if anything, repels you, appalls you, or makes you anxious. If it's snakes or alligators, you're hardly alone in that respect—but extremely few of us have actually been threatened by any wildlife or had a dangerous encounter with them. Our fears, fed in part by too many Hollywood movies portraying horrors in swamplands, create much of the problem. See if you can return home from a swamp with some appreciation and insights.

Deserts

Deserts have a surprising number of passionate advocates, considering all the bad press they've long received. Regardless of their reputation as wastelands, deserts are often home to an unexpected variety of life-forms. Many of these have evolved with defensive aids—such as the sharp thorns and needles found on numerous varieties of vegetation, which discourage potential diners—as well as mechanisms for coping with extreme heat and water scarcity. A number of more conventional species of wildlife and birds also make their homes in the desert.

While it's easy to perceive deserts as hostile and impossibly austere environments, some of them present absolutely spectacular landscapes with magnificent landforms including canyons, mesas, and every conceivable kind of rock formation. Given the minimal rainfall, vegetation is indeed sparse compared with most of the earth's other landscapes, so much of the surface typically consists of naked rock and dry sand.

Spending time in the desert is extremely conducive to barebones thinking: trimming away the frills, eliminating the superfluous, and considering life's essentials. It's no coincidence that saints, ascetics, and prophets often sought the desert for their extended meditations and visions. Nowhere are the gifts of water and life likely to be more appreciated. Nowhere do the excesses of the modern world seem more glaring or our materialistic urges appear to be more misguided.

Visiting a desert calls for extra caution, given the lack of water and the potential for extremely high temperatures. Getting lost or seriously injured some distance from a road could be fatal. Always carry and drink at least a gallon of water per day, avoid strenuous exercise during the hottest hours, and do everything you can to protect yourself from the intense radiation of the sun in this largely shadeless region. Also, never go without a map and compass and the knowledge of how to use them.

To avoid higher temperatures, late fall through spring are the recommended times of year to visit deserts and other semi-arid areas in the western states. Spring is also the wildflower season, when the desert becomes somewhat more colorful and attractive. Be prepared for possible cold temperatures during these seasons, especially at higher elevations and in the evening and nighttime hours. For the coolest temperatures and the greatest likelihood of encountering wildlife, the best times of day to walk or hike in the desert are early morning and evening.

Taking a One-Day Desert Retreat

If you're someone who is capable of finding pleasure in a period of relative inactivity and rest and can find appeal in the idea of a personal retreat, spend a quiet, contemplative day in the desert. You could also walk or hike for a time at the start, but don't venture far by yourself unless you're experienced and well-equipped for desert travel. If it's sunny and hot, be sure to wear a wide-brimmed hat, apply plenty of sunscreen, and carry a gallon or more of water. For reasons of safety, you may even want to stay within sight of your car or a road. Given the open visibility in many arid areas, however, this could still allow you to go in as far as a couple of miles.

After surveying your surroundings, taking a close look at the land and its relatively small number of visible inhabitants, park your body in a spot that offers some shade, if available, or any place that otherwise attracts you. Perhaps there are flowering cacti or other interesting vegetation nearby, or you can find a rock perch from which to view the vast open spaces around you. Maybe an impressive mountain, mesa, or rock formation stands before you and keeps drawing your attention.

Consider why you're here, which could be to take a vacation from work, or to learn more about deserts and other natural areas, or to commune with the earth, or for other reasons. Try to evaluate your feelings about the desert at the start of the day. Are you resisting becoming acquainted with your surroundings, wishing you were someplace lusher, cooler, and more congenial, or are you actually savoring the experience? Let the extreme quiet slowly seep into your consciousness and likewise into the relative emptiness of the spaces around you. The openness here is extraordinary compared with the crowded, indoor world of people that most of us occupy in everyday life, although there are also more living beings here than initially meet the eye.

Breathe deeply of the desert air and exhale any cobwebs, irritations, distractions, and other preoccupations that may be residing in your mind. Allow whatever tensions and stresses you've been holding in your body to be slowly released into the great, receptive space you're enveloped in. Think about what's truly important to you. Consider what may come next in your life. There's no better setting than this spare but soul-welcoming place, free of distractions, for inviting the answers and allowing them to come.

The desert's simplicity and austerity seem to make it easier for us to inwardly "get down to brass tacks"—to get in touch with the deepest essentials in our lives and clarify any confusion we may have about goals, values, and pursuits. Perhaps here we can come closer to realizing our potential for making an enduring spiritual connection with the rest of creation.

18

✺

EXPLORING GEOLOGICAL
FEATURES

WE'RE FORTUNATE TO LIVE on a planet whose face is pock-marked with so many interesting, eye-catching features and landforms. While relatively flat and uniform areas aren't uncommon, the earth's surface also expresses a great amount of geological variability and heterogeneity. It's hard to imagine living in a world without such distinctive features as hills, mountains, cliffs, canyons, caves, and rock formations.

Geological features break up the visual landscape in attractive and sometimes surprising ways that stir our imaginations and inevitably invite exploration. Almost all spectacular or awe-inspiring natural scenery includes such components. It's difficult to be indifferent to the rocky splendor of lofty mountains, for example, or the echoing vastness of great canyons. Landforms seem to stir our minds and encourage us to entertain deeper thoughts and questions. They remind us of the mind-boggling age of the earth, the unimaginable geological events that created some of our most dramatic landscapes, and the all-too-emphemeral nature of our own lives.

Only a minority of us actually live near imposing or striking landforms. We may want to take vacation trips to such sites, but travel isn't mandatory—most of us can also find places of geological interest that are relatively close to home, some of which may be little-known and overlooked. We can learn much from exploring less glamorous sites, and it's always helpful to cultivate an appreciation for local landscapes.

Hills

Small hills are found almost everywhere, even in the so-called flatlands. Their possible origins are many: some consist of glacial debris from the last ice age, others are eroded remnants of higher ground, and still others are man-made, such as ancient burial mounds. Hills lend a pleasant dose of visual interest to the land whatever their size, whether they stand only a few feet high or loom hundreds of feet or more above the surrounding area. When unforested, they serve as convenient vantage points for viewing the local countryside.

To a weary or unenthusiastic pedestrian, a hill may well be an unwelcome obstacle due to the exertion required to ascend it. To the more avidly active and exercise-oriented among us, however, hills positively cry out to be climbed. They urge us to stretch our muscles and allow our pulses to quicken and our breathing to deepen. They invite us to enjoy the "elevated atmosphere" and partake in any available scenic perspectives. Even when dense foliage precludes the possibility of views, walking or hiking across hilly terrain tends to be more interesting, stimulating, and fun than traversing "the flats."

Taking a Hill Walk

Get acquainted with an undeveloped and roadless hill or two in your area. It could be open and grassy, as you'll find in park meadows, grasslands, or on abandoned farmlands, or it might be entirely wooded and wild. Notice the vegetation and keep your eyes open for wildlife, but stay hill-minded: pay attention to the contours of the land as you walk them.

See if you can entirely circumvent the hill at the bottom, assuming no fences, wetlands, or other obstacles block your passage around it. Then try slowly ascending the hill in a spiral until you reach the top. If it's too rocky or steep in places, you could also follow any preexisting path or make your own way. Take a rest break on top, if you're tired, or at any inviting spot you find along the hillside. Then continue to circle, traverse, and explore the hill until you know its shape and feel by heart. Few hills or other landforms, you'll notice, are perfectly symmetrical. Perhaps this is a place to come back to when you're feeling world-weary. If there's a vista, it will usually be an ideal place to watch for raptors and other birds, or to come back to at night for some stargazing.

If other hills are nearby, try wandering from one to another, enjoying the sensuous shapes of the land as you move across it. Notice the shallow or steep depressions, valleys, or ravines that lie between hills; these were probably carved by streams or scoured by a glacier during the last ice age. As you meander through the landscape, be aware that you're exploring the planet's skin, which has been molded into its present form over enormous expanses of time. If you can attune to the living body of the earth beneath your feet, walking these aesthetic surface contours, which sometimes include scars and rough imperfections, can start to feel like an intimate act as well as a sacred one.

Mountains

Mountains are the earth's most majestic landforms. If we're receptive and keep our senses open, we may easily fall under their overpowering spell. Each year mountains draw untold numbers of tourists and outdoorspeople, and frequently they're the destinations for sacred pilgrimages as well. Many people choose to live in or near mountains in order to bask in their magnificence and stunning beauty, to benefit from the cleaner and more rarified air that's common at higher altitudes, and to enjoy the nearly limitless recreational possibilities.

The great mountains are famous for inspiring awe and humility. Their spectacular scale helps keep us in our place, because in their presence it's difficult to maintain an overblown sense of self-importance. At the same time, few places are better to go to than the mountains when we're feeling lost, confused, discouraged, depressed, exhausted, or otherwise out of touch with ourselves or the natural world. Or when we're in need of solitude, a respite from everyday existence, and renewed perspectives. Or when we're looking for greater challenges and loftier goals. In the mountains we're removed from ordinary realities, and if we stay for long we're likely to come face-to-face with some of life's fundamentals. If what we seek includes meaning, hope, or spiritual self-realization, our search could be rewarded here.

It's also important to remember that life doesn't come easy in the mountains, and wisdom always has its price. Extremes of weather and climate are characteristic of many higher mountain areas; a visitor can face severe storms that include lightning, high winds, bitter cold, and other potentially life-threatening conditions at any time. Venturing off the beaten path in the mountains can be especially hazardous, and altitude sickness is a risk. Those who wish to hike or climb major mountains should always do so with an established group and only embark on mountain travel after adequate preparation.

On the other hand, the memorable thrills of exploring mountains can never be discounted, nor can the psychological and spiritual benefits of communing with such splendid and often stupendous rock "beings." Yet you don't need to risk your neck to have a potentially life-changing experience. The superb air and breathtaking vistas alone are sometimes remarkably mind-shifting, and these can often be found along relatively safe trails at somewhat lower elevations and in accessible locations.

It's easy to wax eloquent about the higher mountain ranges such as our Rockies, Sierras, and Cascades, which understandably are revered. But for the purposes of communing with mountains we mustn't ignore the many smaller and sometimes underrated ranges, including the ancient Appalachians and Alleghenies of the East. While less stunning in their stature, such mountains offer easier access, a more human-friendly scale, somewhat safer weather, and everyday availability to people who seek mountain experiences.

Ascending a Mountain

For most of us, climbing a mountain has little in common with what practitioners of the high-risk sport of mountaineering do, which sometimes includes ascending rock walls and precipitous peaks with ropes and other equipment. For us, climbing simply means walking or hiking up a trail that leads to the top. Most mountain regions in the country have designated and marked hiking trails that offer good and reasonably safe footing, although some routes are extremely rough and rocky.

The difficulty of ascending a mountain depends on the amount of elevation you gain and the steepness and ruggedness of the trail. If you climb a few thousand feet or more and the angle of your ascent is steep, the hike is sure to be strenuous and taxing; getting your body to the top will require burning loads of calories. On the other hand, plenty of smaller mountains include relatively easy, gently sloping trails, suitable for anyone who's at least in minimally good shape.

When in doubt, start with the least imposing mountain and eventually work your way up to bigger ones if you're so inclined. It's indeed easy to get hooked on climbing mountains, given the rush that comes with the vigorous exercise, delicious air, and fantastic views available from the top or along the way. To conserve energy and to avoid overtaxing yourself, climb at a slow, steady pace. If you get winded, take short breaks—as little as a minute or two each—to catch your breath. An extended break is always an option if you need it, but it's hard to regain your momentum when climbing if you stop for long. Be ready to turn back if you should find that you're seriously overextended or at the first hints of an impending storm. Always bring a sizable day pack with plenty of water, food, rain gear, safety items, and more clothing than you think you'll need.

Notice the sometimes infinite array of rocks and boulders, which frequently will be covered with vegetation at lower elevations but are often totally exposed higher up. If you study or read about geology, you'll get a better understanding of the different kinds of rocks and how they may have gotten there. It's also interesting to watch how the vegetation changes as you gain elevation. You may progress through several kinds of forest before reaching tundra near the top, although the specifics will vary from one mountain area and region of the country to another.

There aren't many places where you'll feel more on top of the world than on a mountain summit. Nowhere are your thoughts likely to be lighter or more expansive, which seems to reflect the thinner air and open vistas. Once you arrive, assuming it's not too windy or cold on top, you may want to take a long, leisurely break to rest your tired but possibly exhilarated body, enjoy some spectacular views, survey the horizons and the heavens, have lunch or a snack, and perhaps take a nap. Check in with how you feel, and notice how radically different your mood probably is since the start of the day or when you were last at work.

The length of your stay will partly depend on the weather. On a cold or rainy day it'll be difficult to linger for long unless you have a lot of warm and protective clothing. Even so, your instincts will probably tell you to move on soon. On a mild, sunny day, in contrast, chances are you'll want to settle in for a more extended time. A couple of hours usually aren't too long for a mountaintop rest, especially if you're in the mood for thinking or meditating, but be careful to avoid getting too much direct sun. If you're in great shape and your ascent wasn't too difficult, you may be inclined to traverse another peak or two before the day is done. On the other hand, many of us find that our adventurous urges are perfectly satisfied, at least for the time being, by one beautiful mountain.

Canyons

The great canyons are as capable of overwhelming us with their nearly undigestible depth and scale as the most spectacular mountains. Our mile-deep Grand Canyon is the best known of them all, but countless other large canyons, chasms, and gorges cut through the mountain and canyon country of our western states. Many smaller canyons and gorges are found in the East and throughout most of the rest of the United States as well.

Canyons usually have rivers or streams running through them, the same waterways that typically carved out these chasms over the course of unimaginable amounts of time. Peering down into a canyon you can often read the layers of exposed and eroded rock that represent previous eras. Hiking to the depths is a bit like taking a geological journey into the distant past.

In most canyons you'll find an extremely quiet, peaceful atmosphere ideal for solitude—except for the possible noise of planes or helicopters overhead, which unfortunately disrupts our most famous canyons. Trails lead to the bottom of many canyons, and descending on foot is one of the best ways to get a sense of their size. The only catch is that you need to climb back up, so those who aren't very fit should resist any impulse to go more than a short distance down from the top.

Sitting on a canyon rim is a superb place to observe and reflect on the depths, especially when the area isn't crowded with tourists. If it is, park rangers will usually be able to suggest some more isolated locations where you'll find few fellow travelers. Another wonderful way to see a great canyon is to raft through it, which can be a supreme wilderness adventure.

Descending into a Canyon

Locate a reasonably wide and safe trail that will take you down into a canyon. Before descending, you should have at least a rough idea of how far it is to the bottom, which you can find out from a map, guidebook, or park visitor center. Before proceeding all the way down, be sure you're physically capable of climbing back to the top. Use extra caution and restraint in a desert canyon, where it could be extremely hot below. Here you're likely to need a lot of extra water, probably at least a gallon, and the return trip to the top may be especially taxing.

Descending into a canyon or gorge is the reverse of climbing a mountain, and you'll similarly notice changes in the environment as you lose elevation. Examine the visible layers of rocks, which have been exposed by the action of the river or stream below ages ago, as well as by weathering from the elements. In some of our southwestern canyons, in particular, these rocks assume gorgeous reddish brown colors that seem to radiate light.

As you go down, the vegetation tends to change with the elevation, becoming more sparse in desert areas and lusher elsewhere,
especially as you approach water. In larger canyons, different
wildlife may occupy the lower elevations.

If it's feasible, continue walking until you get to the stream
or river that runs through the canyon (assuming there is one and
it's not dry). Take your longest rest break there. Enjoy the lovely
sounds of water breaking the deep, peaceful silence. Appreciate
the protective, sheltering presence of the canyon walls. Resume
your return trip back to the top while plenty of daylight hours
still remain, allowing extra time for the required exertion and
for possible discoveries along the way.

Cliffs

Open cliffs cap canyon walls, project from mountainsides, and
are situated in many other locations where rock is exposed or
elevated, which includes many of the flatter, nonmountainous
regions of the country. Hiking trails often lead to and cross cliffs,
which make for ideal rest spots. They're perfect perches for surveying the countryside and the lay of the land, studying clouds,
watching for raptors and other birds, stretching out for naps,
and contemplating anything and everything under the sun.

Given how exposed they are, cliffs are often subject to brisk
winds, so you may need to bring some extra clothing along if the
day is cool and you want to spend much time there. Like a
mountaintop, a cliff is no place to be in a storm; lightning strikes
are a serious risk, as they are in any prominent place higher than
the surrounding terrain. So it's wise to promptly get off the cliff

and head for a more protected area at the first hint of a thunderstorm or other severe weather.

Caves

Under the earth in some regions are amazing networks of caves, the most famous of which have hundreds of miles of passages as well as enormous, strangely colored caverns with bizarre formations that present an absolutely otherworldly appearance. A few are protected as national parks or developed as private tourist attractions, and these often include such amenities as elevators, lighted walkways, and guided tours.

Most caves are more ordinary and less spectacular than these, but they're still of interest to those who are drawn to explore the darker recesses of the planet's surface. The sport or hobby of spelunking is devoted to just such explorations. Caves and open crevices that can be entered are found in many mountain areas, canyons, hillsides, and elsewhere.

Because of potential dangers, which include falling, getting lost, or even drowning in underground waterways, entry points to caves on public lands are often blocked off or concealed. Casual explorers should be well aware of the risks and go only with a guide or an organized group. Although most of us limit ourselves to aboveground activities, exploring an accessible cave or two can be fun. It's fascinating to know that beneath us is an entirely different world, which in some areas includes huge networks and mazes of passages and chambers. Some caves deep beneath the surface or far from possible points of entry have yet to be visited by any human being.

Rock Formations

Rock underlies much of the land, and where it's been thrust up, exposed, fractured, or weathered by the elements, it's capable of taking on a seemingly infinite number of forms. Some of our national parks feature or include scores of eye-arresting rock formations, spires, pinnacles, arches, and natural bridges, many of which are enormous, striking, and amazing to witness in person. Such formations are also scattered across other public and private lands throughout much of the country, although the majority of these are on a much smaller scale.

The exposed rock speaks volumes about its past, and we need to turn to geology to fully interpret and understand the messages. But even if we know little about their origins, it's still impressive, captivating, and thought-provoking to experience the aesthetic shapes and forms of rock in such unexpected and unlikely arrangements. Our interest tends to be aroused and our imagination stimulated. Here, once again, the earth reminds us that physical existence includes a great deal more than the flat, visually predictable, and canned world we've made for ourselves in modern times; that the planetary platform upon which life and nature unfold and express themselves is almost infinitely variable and unique; and that the face of the earth probably holds more mysteries, material and spiritual, than any of us would be able to unravel in a multitude of lifetimes.

19

⌒∞⌒

EXPERIENCING
THE ELEMENTS

OUTSIDE OF OUR CLIMATE-CONTROLLED environments reigns the ever-changing and often unpredictable weather, which sometimes appears to have a mind of its own—and has succeeded thus far in defeating our attempts to subdue it. Many of us habitually complain about the weather, which is another indication of our alienation from natural forces. We're unaware of how important weather-related processes are to life on earth.

Granted, the elements can make things uncomfortable for us, especially if we don't know how to dress for them or protect ourselves from their extremes. They're notorious for periodically unraveling our plans and inconveniencing us, which we modern folk—addicted as we are to our schedules and agendas—find increasingly intolerable. Yet the weather's unexpected turns and excesses may also benefit us by teaching us the value of patience, flexibility, and delayed gratification, as well as the gift of unexpected free time.

But the weather by no means exists for our sake, which may be another reason why some of us find the unreliability of the elements and our inability to influence them so irritating; we want to have some say in the process. We need to be reeducated about the role of the weather and reminded that it's part of the climatic scheme of things under which life has evolved and flourished here on earth. The purposes weather serves include redistributing water across the land. Without precipitation, the majority of flora and fauna couldn't survive, including many of the species we depend on for food.

Those of us who are adaptable and thrive on variety are more likely to actually appreciate and enjoy the weather with its many surprises. Climatic and temperature fluctuations require a number of adjustments from us, but if we're reasonably flexible these can be experienced as stimulating and even exhilarating. The weather makes life in and out of nature more interesting.

No one, however, takes lightly the fact that extreme weather occasionally harms or kills people and destroys property. Statistics verify that hurricanes and other dangerous storms are on the increase, and this appears to be not a sign of "merciless nature" but rather a human-created problem related to global warming. We're continuing to release enormous amounts of carbon dioxide and other gases into the atmosphere, causing it to heat up and creating conditions more conducive to severe weather. Projections by climatologists are for a greater incidence of catastrophic storms in the future unless we drastically reduce emissions. Thus while extreme weather will probably always be

with us on a limited scale, it appears that we could help reduce
its frequency and severity by learning to live in more ecologically sustainable ways.

Rain

Few elements are more essential to the ecosystem than rain. This
life-giving process helps to continuously recycle water and return
it to the land, where it's so greatly needed. The water initially
evaporates from oceans, lakes, and wetlands; forms clouds; then
is eventually released and dispersed via storms, showers, and
other precipitation. In this way the rain meets the water needs
of countless living things, ourselves included.

The amount of bad press rain and the other elements have
received in modern times is unfortunate. Our media and the
culture at large are in the habit of bad-mouthing all precipitation, creating negative expectations for us. The expression
"bad weather" may indeed be appropriate for tornadoes, hurricanes, and other truly severe storms, but it's now often
stretched to cover the lightest mist, the briefest shower, and
everything else that falls short of perfectly clear, sunny, blue-sky
weather.

However, let the rain stop altogether for a few months or
years, as happens during droughts, and watch the results. At
such times we witness how absolutely essential the rain is to our
existence and how misguided our negativity and lack of gratitude for it is. Droughts have been occurring with increasing frequency in recent years, as part of a worldwide climatic upheaval;
the effects have been devastating to many species. But only when

it touches us directly, as when human communities run out of water, do we see and feel how totally dependent we are on the rainfall. If it fails, we're in big trouble. We simply must have it to live.

You can appreciate rain's value without necessarily choosing to spend time out in it—although if you commune with nature or participate in outdoor activities, you're almost certain to get caught in it occasionally. But why do we have a problem with rain in the first place? After all, it's only water, the same liquid we like or love in other contexts. One reason is that we can't control it, which we find perpetually annoying in our zeal to run the show. Thus too many of us have been taught from an early age to hate or fear the rain. If that's true for you, it may be time to work on your attitude. Contrary to what many of us were told as children, rain won't make you sick—that is, as long as you avoid getting chilled in it, which is easily done by wearing the right clothing and rainwear. Rain can't ruin your day if you don't want it to. And cursing rain is like cursing life.

Considering how negatively our culture tends to view most precipitation, a surprising number of us have learned to enjoy going out in it. Walking in the rain in warm weather can even be a sensuous experience. Many of us who love nature know how beautiful the natural world frequently appears in the rain—in contrast with cities, which tend to be gray and grim when they're wet. The only important precondition for being out in the rain is knowing how to dress for it. Staying dry isn't as important when temperatures are high, but in cooler weather you need some waterproof rain gear to keep the rain off your body, plus enough additional clothing to stay warm and comfortable.

Taking a Walk in the Rain

If it's not already an occasional practice for you, and the idea doesn't strike you as absurd, try taking a pleasure walk in the rain. A natural setting is preferable, where precipitation seems most at home anyway. Make sure you're properly dressed for it. On a cool or cold day, do your best to wear little or no cotton, especially next to your skin, to reduce any chances that you'll get chilled; choose synthetics, silk, or wool instead. Wear footwear that's waterproof or at least water resistant, if possible. Check in with your feelings and thoughts before and during the walk, and notice whether you're at all inclined to rush and get it over with; try to take your time and savor the experience. Remember that any outing can always be shortened or terminated if you find yourself experiencing serious discomfort that you can't correct.

Keep your senses wide open as you walk, observing the glistening plant world as it drinks in the rain. Make note of what in nature attracts you now, and note whether you find anything unappealing about these conditions. What scents can you detect? How intense are they? Keep an eye out for salamanders and other little creatures that may be crawling about. Feel the wetness on any exposed skin and the soggy earth beneath your feet.

Stop periodically to rest, either standing or sitting, perhaps under the semi-shelter of a tree (avoid lone standing trees during an electrical storm). Give the rain your undivided attention for a time. Watch the mist, light rain, or deluge as it descends. Listen closely. The sounds will vary depending on how hard the rain is coming down. In a shower you'll usually hear the hissing of thousands of raindrops hitting the leaves of trees, bushes, rocks, and the earth, as well as splattering in puddles. Is the effect relaxing? Or do you feel anxious and uneasy? Can you imagine finding enjoyment, fun, and excitement in being caught out in a surprise shower or storm?

Snow

Precipitation is never lovelier than when it arrives in the airy, almost otherworldly form of snow, which beautifully coats trees, bushes, and man-made structures in white. Snow utterly transforms the winter landscape, sometimes assuming fantastic forms as it drifts in the wind across the land's features. When the sun comes out we may be transfixed by the glittering snow. Even those who are resolutely indoor-oriented and winter-resistant often admire the ethereal beauty of snowscapes.

Whether it's falling or already on the ground, snow invites our participation and exploration. Children know instinctively how to have fun in it. You don't have to go more than a few feet from your home to enjoy it, and all you need are some warm and preferably snow-resistant clothing and boots. Snow can provide almost limitless opportunities for nature-based adventures. If the snow is deep enough, two especially effective and pleasurable ways to get around in it are on snowshoes and cross-country skis.

Fresh snow and sleet do tend to impede road travel, which is one reason why they're seen in such a negative light by some of us who must rely on our cars to get to work and elsewhere. Driving becomes potentially dangerous when roads are snow-covered and absolutely treacherous when they're icy. When in doubt, we may be better off staying home and enjoying a day off—the perfect time for venturing out into the snow in our winter boots, on snowshoes, or on cross-country skis.

Taking a Snow Walk

Going for a walk in the snow is almost always a good idea, and it's the simplest way for us to get some fresh air, exercise, and a taste of nature in winter. When the snow is new or still coming down, it tends to be especially lovely and enticing. If the snow is deep and you don't have snowshoes or Nordic skis on hand, walking is sure to be strenuous exercise, so you may not want to venture far. In shallow or compacted snow, the going will be much easier. Feel the snow's consistency under your feet—ranging from hard or crunchy to soft or slushy—which varies with the air temperature and how compressed the snow is.

Even the shortest snow walk in nature should provide plenty to see. Look for icicles, ice formations, and other ice crystals. Notice how bushes, smaller tree branches, and other vegetation bend from the weight of a coating of ice or snow. Stop to study the snow close up and see if you can perceive individual crystals. One of the best places to pick them out is on your clothing when it's snowing. When the snow is coming down hard, it's like being inside a massive waterfall of flakes. Spend some time watching them descend from the heavens. If you're dressed warmly enough to sit for a few minutes or more and take in the show from a stationary position, it can be as mesmerizing and relaxing as sitting in front of a waterfall in spring or summer. Feel some of the snowflakes melt on your face.

Snow seems to visually unify and unite the two separate worlds of nature and civilization for a time by blanketing everything with crystals. (Snowplows and snowblowers, however, are quickly put to work in the human realm in an attempt to reassert our dominance over the natural.) Visiting wild nature in the snow is like entering a giant, silent, soft womb of white. While it may be outwardly cold, the snow offers insulation and protection to the flora and fauna bedded down beneath it. Look for signs of wildlife, which are often clearly written in the snow.

One of the hazards of going out at this time of year is the possibility of taking a fall. If you should slip or otherwise start to lose your balance, don't resist falling. Simply try to plop down on your rear end. If that's impossible, use your hands to carefully break your fall, or roll over as you land in the snow. If there's enough snow, it usually provides sufficient cushioning to keep you from getting hurt. When there's ice, which is much more unforgiving to the human body, you're wise to proceed especially slowly and cautiously, or return home and postpone your walk until another time. The only truly safe way to walk on ice-covered walkways or paths is with crampons (metal devices with spikes that are strapped onto your boots).

It's also vital to avoid getting lost in the wild at this time of year, which could be life-threatening. Visibility is extremely limited when it's snowing hard, and you may find it difficult to stay oriented. Never count on following your footprints back to the road or your house, since fresh or windblown snow could easily cover and obscure your tracks. Remember, the weather can change abruptly in winter just as at other times of year. You could start a long walk with fair skies overhead and end up finishing it a couple of hours later in a blizzard. Whenever taking more than a short excursion, always bring a map, compass, and a day pack with water, some food, extra clothing, first aid items, and other emergency supplies.

Winds and Breezes

There are times and places where the air remains absolutely still, but this invisible element is more often on the move. Ranging from ferocious storm winds to barely detectable breezes, the weather-inducing layer of air that surrounds the earth is forever stirring things up. Winds wreak havoc when their velocities are fiercest, as in hurricanes and tornadoes, and biting winds chill us to the bone in cold weather if we're inadequately dressed. Yet breezes also provide wonderful fair-weather refreshment, helping to keep us comfortably cool in times of summer heat.

During the warmer seasons we're likely to experience winds and breezes as sensuous, stirring, evocative, and otherwise attractive. Nature's aliveness seems accentuated by the tossing to and fro of tree branches and boughs in the wind, by trembling bushes and rippling grasses, and by lake whitecaps and oceanside surf. Breezes and winds lend an intensified sense of living presence to the land, a strong hint of spiritual habitation.

Entering the Wind

Pick a windy or breezy day for a walk in the woods or to traverse an open natural area. Along the way, find a suitable spot where you can sit for a time. Listen attentively to the wind or breeze as it sweeps or brushes across the landscape, whistling through pine boughs, swooshing through small bushes, whispering through tall grasses, and perhaps rustling dead leaves. Try to identify the sources of the different sounds it makes as it comes in contact with the various elements of nature.

Watch, too, how the wind buffets tree branches, bushes, and other vegetation and moves them in rhythmic ways, causing them to bend, swing, and dance. Leaves will usually flutter wildly in a stiff wind, with a few of them sometimes taking flight with each gust. In autumn they may absolutely rain down on you. If you're near a lake or pond, notice how the wind stirs the water and creates waves or ripples. Feel the currents of air caress your body as well. Let the wind massage your exposed skin, toss your hair, and ruffle any loose clothing. The ebbs and gusts are almost like the atmosphere itself breathing in and out. Can you absorb any of this invigorating energy as it envelops you?

Storms

Although we may get caught out in a severe storm on occasion, most of us don't choose to be outside in such conditions if we can help it. Given the potential danger, it's only sensible to stay home or at least seek protection when a storm clearly is brewing. There's a big and obvious difference, however, between routine thunderstorms and catastrophic storms like hurricanes. Some of us live in areas where afternoon thunderstorms are almost a daily occurrence in summertime, and there's no need to retreat inside as long as we're vigilant regarding lightning. Whenever an electrical storm is likely, it's important to avoid mountaintops, hilltops, lakeshores, open fields, and other exposed areas where we might be the tallest figures around. And we should never seek shelter under a lone tree. If we're in a forest at lower elevations, though, the chances of being struck by lightning are miniscule.

Another possible storm hazard is having debris, including tree branches or occasionally the trees themselves, rain down on us. If winds are high it's best to seek the closest available shelter, which in a wilderness area might be a cave or rock overhang. Be aware as well of the possibility of flooding from heavy rains, which can quickly swell small streams and turn them into impassable, raging torrents—temporarily stranding any hikers or other backcountry travelers in the wild.

While sometimes scary, storms can also be experienced as exciting and fascinating. With suitable rain gear and clothing, and exercising the appropriate precautions, it can be exhilarating to be out in a storm. We shouldn't take foolish chances, but witnessing a storm can be inspiring. The stupendous display of weather and the raw power and unleashed forces of nature can give us an overdue dose of humility. Seeing a storm blow through also makes for a fantastic show. Afterward the air is often extraordinarily clear and clean, and when the sun reemerges, it may momentarily seem as if the world has been reborn.

Cold

Frigid weather is about as popular with the majority of us as rainy weather, but a significant number of outdoor enthusiasts become passionate advocates and aficionados of cold-weather activities. The cold may initially seem intimidating, but it can also be thoroughly invigorating and stimulating. And the natu-

ral world has far fewer visitors in the colder seasons, so we'll usually find as much solitude and quiet as we want.

If we head indoors whenever the temperature drops, as many
people do, we may be cutting ourselves off from nature for up
to several months each year. It's worth trying to make friends
with the cold and work through our fears about it, which can
free us up to enjoy a number of possible winter activities out in
the natural world. We'll also be much less likely to fall victim to
winter blues or cabin fever. While many life-forms are dormant
and hidden under the snow, there's still much of interest to discover in the wild during the coldest season. We owe it to ourselves to stay connected to nature at this time of year.

The key to being comfortable in the cold is mastering the art
of dressing for it. Never skimp on the clothing you bring, even
if you'll be doing some heat-producing aerobic activity. If it's
windy and colder than expected or when you take breaks, you
may need much more protection than you thought. Layering has
long been the recommended way of dressing: start out with at
least several thinner layers of clothing rather than one or two
heavy garments; shed or add layers as soon as you feel overheated
or cold; and avoid cotton, especially next to your skin. Always
bring a day pack to carry extra clothing and other items. And
make sure you have good protection for your extremities, including heavy gloves or mittens for your hands, a knitted cap or
other warm hat, and in subzero cold, a face mask.

Note your reactions to the cold when you go out in winter,
particularly if you're aware of negative thoughts and feelings.
There are always actions you can take if you're uncomfortable
in any way, such as putting on more clothing or retreating to a
warm building if necessary. But as long as you're warm enough,

you'll find few limits to your enjoyment and as much freedom as you want to experience nature in the cold.

Exploring the Cold

Spend some time wandering in the wild during a cold snap, whether or not there's snow on the ground, and pay special attention to your reactions and responses to the cold. Wear appropriate clothing and bring some extra items in a day pack. Add or remove layers as soon as necessary to remain comfortably warm without overheating. If you're starting to sweat, stop and take off some layers; and whenever you feel cold or chilled, promptly put a few layers back on.

Feel the cold on the skin of your face (which in extreme cold you should cover with a face mask, especially on windy days, but this is ordinarily unnecessary in above-zero temperatures). To what extent does the cold seem like an adversary or a dangerous element? How successfully, with the assistance of clothing, is your body adapting to it? Do you find dealing with the cold a challenge? Or is it a pleasure? Can you detect any hints of inner exhilaration budding in the face of some bracing cold?

The more you can make friends with the cold, feel relaxed in the outdoors during frigid weather, and comfortably acclimate to the lowest temperatures, the better you'll be able to stay attuned to nature during the coldest months—as well as relate to natural climatic swings and cycles, including weather extremes. The cold deserves some healthy respect, but it can also teach us about adaptation, using "adversity" to strengthen ourselves, and freeing ourselves from self-imposed limits. Cold conditions can also assist us in learning to commune more deeply with the multifaceted elements of nature that we too often perceive to be hostile or unsavory.

Heat

Our bodies are just as capable of acclimating to higher temperatures as to lower ones. It's true that extreme heat can be taxing to us, but in time our bodies will begin to adjust to it. One problem is that many of us occupy and are adjusted to air-conditioned environments, so our bodies rarely have any opportunity to fully accommodate to hot weather.

When you go out in the heat it's especially important to drink hefty amounts of water—as much as a gallon or more during the day, especially in the desert—to avoid dehydration. You need to replenish all the water you lose through sweating, which is your body's method of preventing overheating. During a spell of heat or in a sweltering environment, it's also wise to limit any strenuous exercise to early and late in the day. Try to restrict your direct exposure to the sun and remain in the shade whenever possible. When you can't avoid the sun, wearing a wide-brimmed hat and ample amounts of sunscreen are important. It's also helpful to wet a bandanna with cool water and keep mopping your brow, and to periodically wet your shirt and other clothing as well. If you start to feel the least bit dizzy or weak it's important to rest, and if necessary, cut short the physical activity.

Outdoor heat can be pleasurable as long as it doesn't overwhelm the body's ability to maintain an appropriate temperature. Few things are more delightful and sensual after an extended excursion into nature than taking a hot bath or sauna, and natural heat can feel just as good on our skin when we're still in the wild. The ultimate source of all heat is always our sun, without which life could never have originated here on earth in the first place—nor could it continue on for much longer. Human body temperature must be maintained just a bit below 100 degrees Fahrenheit, which is rather warm. Aside from the discomfort that high humidity sometimes causes, most of us can still learn to be reasonably contented in the heat.

Becoming at Home in the Heat

How much we prefer or dislike hot weather usually has something to do with where we grew up and how much time we've spent in the heat. The wider the range and variety of conditions we can learn to be at home in, the better off we are. Otherwise our lives are mostly at the mercy of outside forces, and we're at risk of spending too much of our time avoiding, griping about, or otherwise feeling discontented with the climate and weather.

Go out into nature on a hot day, carrying a large supply of water, avoiding direct sunlight as much as you can, and using restraint with exercise except for early and late in the day. Sit or lie down in a comfortable place. Feel the waves of heat enveloping you and the sun-based energy they're bringing you; breathe in deeply of this powerful medicine. If you've recently been in air-conditioned spaces or are acclimated to cooler weather, the heat may feel enervating and depleting at first. But in time you may notice that this form of energy seems to stimulate the cells of your body and may even cause your skin to tingle. Keep an inventory of your feelings and sensations. Observe any unusual thoughts, insights, or other interesting inner experiences. Allow the heat to infuse you, enliven you, and inflame you. Perhaps it'll assist in awakening some of the frozen or sleeping parts of your psyche.

20

⚜

OPENING OURSELVES

TO THE SKY

THE ULTIMATE CEILING over our heads is furnished by the great celestial dome of the sky, which harbors a life-giving sun, a tide-pulling moon, and our galaxy's glittering snowscape of stars. For earth-based peoples of the past and present the sky has exerted a constant, overarching presence, and it has served as an important source of guidance to those who could read its ever-shifting signs. It remains to some of us an inspiring and unimaginably vast realm of unfathomable mysteries.

Many of us now pay little attention to the sky, however, except perhaps for an occasional upward glance to verify the weather on our way to work. In some developed areas the sky has practically disappeared behind tall buildings and smog-laden air. We tend to be too busy to look up anyway, so focused are we on our endless earthly preoccupations. It takes a full moon, or a spectacular sunset, or an eclipse, or a comet, or unusual weather to coax us into elevating our eyes to the heavens.

The sky is our visual gateway to the rest of the universe, and in our hubris we sometimes forget we're only an infinitesimally small part of the whole. It's helpful to have some idea of just where our planet fits into the solar system, galaxy, and greater universe. The heavens provide vital reference points for us, making it easier to locate ourselves within the greatest of all possible contexts. Whenever we're attempting to connect with nature we shouldn't fail to consider the seemingly infinite universe we're situated within, nor forget what a rare and precious commodity life is amid the vast reaches of space.

We can visually relate to the sky almost anytime we're outdoors, although in cities we may need to crane our necks to see it. We can also view a bit of sky from our windows when we're indoors. Whether we're in the wild, at home, or even stuck in a traffic jam, taking a few moments or more to survey, study, or contemplate the heavens is always worthwhile.

Scanning the Sky

The wider and more natural the vistas available to us for sky-watching, the better. When the sky is framed by trees, water, and other natural elements, sky-gazing will usually be more relaxing and inspiring. Find a grassy clearing in the woods, a nice stretch of beach, or any reasonably open area where you can take in a good portion of the sky. Your backyard may do if you live in a suburb, small town, or the country. In a city your best bet will usually be the nearest sizable park.

Stretch out on the ground or on a reclining chair, or find a comfortable spot to sit where you can lean your head back without getting a stiff neck. You could bring a pillow for your head if you like and perhaps a foam pad for the rest of your body, although having direct contact with the ground is preferable. Let the sky completely fill your eyes. Unless you live in an area where the weather is uniform, you're likely to see a different scene every day. Some days the sky will be sunny and absolutely clear; others it may be partly or entirely cloudy, with different kinds of clouds and degrees of brightness; still others it'll probably be precipitating, in which case you may want to stay indoors. Or you could bravely don some rainwear and spend some time studying the rainy, misty, or snowy sky.

Clouds

Clouds are like ethereal intermediaries between the earth and the heavens. They float and drift along at various elevations and sometimes touch down, as in foggy weather. They also periodically release their moisture in the form of rain or other precipitation, giving birth to some of the basic elements discussed in Chapter 19.

The dreamy, easygoing pursuit of cloud-watching was probably enjoyed by our most ancient hominid predecessors. Those who have dared to seriously indulge in such an activity in the modern era have always risked being labeled as lazy by their more industrious neighbors. The experience is not unlike spending some downtime watching water moving slowly by in a stream or waves lapping at a lakeshore. Although it'll hardly appeal to those who are hooked on intense stimulation, for the rest of us it's a visually interesting yet low-key, meditative, relaxation-inducing activity. The potential effects of this "mindless" pursuit, when practiced for intervals away from the buzz of everyday endeavors, include fostering creative thinking.

Contemplating Clouds

Allow clouds to enter your gaze and drift through it. Watch them slowly form and disperse. But don't stare or try to accomplish anything. Relax your eyes as much as possible and let go of any tension. Notice the ever-shifting array of shapes that sometimes are sharply defined, while at other times are amorphous. In a sense, their boundaries are illusory and only last for moments before dissolving into new shapes. Never will they be precisely reproduced. Perhaps clouds mirror ever-changing life itself. We easily become attached to forms, and it's hard for us to let go of them when they grow, metamorphose, and die or are transformed.

Let the clouds float through your mind and invite them to stimulate your imagination. If you happen to have some difficult problems to solve, you may see or read some possible answers in the clouds' perpetual reformulations. If your responsibilities are weighing heavily, try imagining your cares are like clouds, and allow the breezes to carry them far beyond the horizon. If you're facing some daunting challenges, imagine that you and your life are somehow cloud-light so you can move up over or pass around or through the obstacles. Lightening up is indeed something many of us need to do. While there are no guarantees as to outcome, it never hurts to daydream and let our thoughts run free. Sometimes contemplating such natural forms as clouds will elicit unexpected ideas, solutions, or insights.

The Sun

Without our sun there could be no life on earth. Thus we have ample grounds for feeling and expressing gratitude for this fiery orb that will always be our primary source of energy. But it's not merely such an awareness of the sun's importance that has created so many sun-worshipers; basking in the sun's rays has always been a pleasurable experience for human beings and other creatures. Our love for the sun has been dampened in modern times by the dangers of excess exposure, especially due to the thinning ozone layer. This doesn't mean we can no longer enjoy the warmth of the sun, but we need to be careful to cover up or use sunscreen during the times and seasons when the sun's rays are most direct, especially at higher elevations. The sun is also the one celestial body that we must not look at directly without some protection for our eyes.

Although sunbathing is no longer considered to be a safe activity because of skin cancer risks, we can still enjoy sunning ourselves for relatively short stints. We shouldn't deprive ourselves of the important physiological and psychological benefits of full-spectrum sunlight, which is reflected in the feeling of well-being that so many people experience while spending time in the sun.

Even those who are in the habit of ignoring the sky, including more than a few city-dwellers, aren't likely to be oblivious to the sun. It has an inevitable impact on our moods and the visual world outdoors, including the brightness of colors and the clarity with which we see things. We're all also aware of the effect the sun has on air temperatures, including how warm and comfortable our bodies feel when we're outside.

Get to know the trajectory of the sun as it crosses the sky each day, and notice how the path changes with each season. On hazy days you'll sometimes be able to safely look right at it. Whenever it's visible the sun will tell you the relative time of day, which is useful information if you ever find yourself without a watch, especially in the wild.

Watching Sunsets and Sunrises

The appeal of colorful sunsets is universal, and just before the sun dips below the horizon you can often observe it directly. On camping trips, vacations, and sometimes at the beach, watching sunsets becomes a lovely ritual many of us participate in at the end of fair-weather days. Sunsets seem to suggest or be associated with feelings of joy, love, and appreciation for life. For a few minutes, time appears to practically stop; here's one occasion when even hyperactive people can stay still for a bit, especially when the colors are brilliant. Even less dramatic sunsets can make for special moments. The quiet space of a sunset also provides a perfect time to stop and acknowledge the accomplishments and pleasures of the day, and to let go of and leave behind any recent disappointments or worries.

Far fewer of us experience the enjoyment of watching sunrises than sunsets because of the early hours involved. Many people are up and about during predawn hours only on workdays, when they're too busy to take time out for the sun. But you can never go wrong by making room for a sunrise, which is easiest if you turn in early. It's truly a special time when the first, faintest hints of light appear, well before the sun begins to peek above the horizon—which for the majority of us means above hills, trees, houses, or other buildings. This peaceful time is an ideal occasion for setting some positive goals or expectations for the day.

The Moon

In cityscapes the moon and stars are easily lost or drowned out by streetlights and brightly lit buildings, whereas in the countryside the moon still dominates the night sky. Many of us can't resist pausing for a few moments of moonlit contemplation when we catch sight of it shining down from high above our houses or the treetops. We may also want to check its nightly progress from our windows. And it's not unusual to be briefly awakened from our sleep by moonbeams striking our faces and eyes.

The moon has long evoked romance and fantasy for human beings, which hasn't diminished in the least for us with the moon landings of several decades ago. This important sphere continues to cast considerable influence on our planet. As mentioned in Chapter 9, the moon not only affects tides but also our hormonal cycles, creativity, and a range of other behavior.

Meditating on the Moon

Spend some time watching and meditating on the moon, which is easiest to do outdoors on a warm evening. A camping trip is a wonderful occasion for following the course of the moon throughout those evening and nighttime hours when we're awake and allowing the luminescent sphere to keep us company at night. The moon is also sometimes faintly visible in the sky during the day.

A full moon is naturally likely to make a much brighter and more powerful impact on us than the sliver of a new moon. But for observation or meditation it doesn't matter what phase the moon is in. When it's full, it illuminates the land so brightly that you won't need a flashlight to get around. On a clear night the full moon can practically offer enough light to read by.

As in all other natural contexts, it's worth tuning in to your feelings and bodily sensations every now and then while moon-watching. Much more wisdom and information can be found inside our bodies and minds than we ordinarily acknowledge, including intuitive information that many of us fail to respect and have learned to ignore. While there may be no way to prove that the moon affects how you feel, it's interesting to notice certain changes or differences in your perceptions and feelings in its presence. You can draw your own conclusions, as you're the one and only expert when it comes to your experiences.

Try sitting or lying comfortably on the ground and gazing up at the moon, observing its trajectory and infinitely slow progress while allowing thoughts to enter and pass through your mind as they will. Or assume a posture of sitting meditation, gently watching the moon in soft focus while following your breathing. Either way, spending some hours unwinding and simply "being" will usually benefit us in any natural setting, and attending or attuning to the moon will sometimes make for a surprisingly rewarding evening. Maybe nothing important will occur that you can report to others, and there's always the risk that you'll be bored, but then again, you might find your time beneath the moon to be a special and memorable experience.

The Stars

They're sometimes overshadowed by the moon and often obliterated by light pollution, but the stars are nonetheless capable of riveting our attention when we allow ourselves to be captivated by them. They're most likely to intervene into our awareness on clear nights, when we're outdoors in unlit surroundings, including sometimes when we emerge from our cars or houses. A star-studded sky is rarely other than a stirring sight.

The more open and unobstructed the sky is, the better for stargazing. While we can study the sky in a piecemeal way with a limited vista, we really need a wide-screen panoramic view to get a sense of the vastness of space and the seemingly infinite population of stars. If we're emotionally and otherwise receptive to it, the prospect can actually take our breath away and bring goose bumps, or chills to our spine, or tears to our eyes.

You may want to learn the names of constellations and to identify individual stars; courses that teach about the night sky are offered at planetariums and elsewhere. Star maps are also available that you could bring along and examine with a flashlight. A major drawback of using artificial sources of light, however, is that they'll keep your eyes from completely adjusting to the dark; your pupils won't open as wide as they can. To see the most, leave the light off for a half hour or more after arriving at the place where you're going to stargaze.

Aside from the pleasure, inspiration, and information provided by the night sky, a major benefit of becoming more familiar with the moon and stars is that you'll probably come to feel more at home outdoors in the dark, which can help increase your overall level of comfort in the natural world. Fear of the dark is widespread, but it won't stand up well to any serious attempts you make to befriend the night sky.

Looking to the Stars

Clear nights are ideal for surveying the heavens; partly cloudy conditions will often be adequate as well. The wilder and less developed the area you've selected or find yourself in, the better—not only because natural surroundings are appealing, but because in and around inhabited areas light pollution will intervene and greatly reduce the visibility of many stars.

Stretching out on your back is always the best way to view the night sky. Since dew is often on the ground during the evening and nighttime hours, you may want to bring a plastic sheet, foam pad, or waterproof parka to lie on. Having some warm clothing along is also advisable, even in summer, in case it gets cool.

Slowly scan the sky, or let your eyes go where they will. Don't strain to see individual stars, which will become brighter and infinitely more numerous as the evening progresses, the sky darkens, and your eyes adjust. Watch for shooting stars, which will sometimes flash across the sky in an instant. You'll probably also observe the distant lights of airplanes and satellites slowly passing every now and then.

Sharing a quiet, starlit evening with friends or loved ones offers a host of simple pleasures. And this is one of the best settings for addressing and discussing some of life's deepest questions. It can also be a time and place to reflect in solitude on what existence is all about, what your life means, and how you may be linked with nature and the rest of the universe. Dare to let the harder questions come. But allow yourself, as well, to feel and experience the ineffable joy of being alive. Try to embrace the wonder of it all. Stay as long as you can, enjoying the shelter of the stars, the support of the living earth, and the companionship of nature's community; it's a magical combination.

Epilogue

AWAKENING TO NATURE means altering or transforming your relationship to life itself. If you're among the tens of millions of people who spend most of their days indoors, embedded in the man-made world, it's to be expected that your concept of life will largely be human-centered. When you begin weaving more of nature into your everyday existence, however, your sense of life may open up to encompass the much richer, more complex, more communal, and more timeless universe that you're actually part of.

Ending your separation from the rest of the living world could easily put your life on a new course. And the more isolated you've been from the natural realm, the more radically your life may change when you connect in meaningful ways to nature. At the very least, interesting or even extraordinary experiences await you, assuming you're willing and able to go deeply into communion with the natural world.

Awakening to nature means living each day more fully and with increased awareness. It means feeling and sensing the planet's pulsing aliveness. It means becoming conscious of countless other beings and attuning to their energies and qualities. It also means understanding that all living things have their place in the ecosystem, that our existence depends on the survival and well-being of other fauna and flora, and that these species have as much of a right to be here as we do.

When we awaken to nature we can still participate fully and joyfully in the human world—including our modern culture's incredible creations and ever-changing entertainments—if we wish to do so. We may find, in fact, that our enjoyment of everyday pursuits is intensified following the stimulating experiences nature often offers us—although the more artificial and frantic aspects of civilized life are likely to lose their appeal.

Awakening to nature means, in part, fulfilling our rich potential as human beings. All evidence suggests that we were never meant to be totally removed from the natural world, stuffed into small spaces, stuck in chairs, to breathe stagnant air or stare into our computer and TV screens for endless hours. Evolution is open-ended, and no one can say what's in store for us in the long run, but it seems that our species has taken a few wrong turns and is headed in some unhealthy directions.

Awakening to nature is sure to alter the course of our lives in positive and fulfilling ways. Those of us who trust our intuition, the often quiet messages we receive from our body-mind-spirit, usually discover that connecting with nature feels like an essential need. It's as natural for human beings as breathing, eating, sleeping, socializing, and making love. Honoring this primal need nourishes our spirits and souls.

While awakening to nature can bring endless benefits and doses of bliss to our lives, it also has an undeniably painful component: we inevitably become more aware of the consequences of the ecological devastation that's occuring throughout our world. The more we learn to relate to, identify with, and empathize with other living things, the more strongly and personally we may start to take their suffering.

Developing special sensitivity to nature's splendors and energies makes it increasingly difficult to witness the poisoning and other violence that's perpetrated against our "relations" in the natural world. Environmental destruction is, of course, taking place at this very moment in countless locations, which may include some places near where you live. You won't witness it all personally, and the media reports on only a small portion of the damage, but it's continuing right now at a rate that's disastrous for the future of most living things.

Our culture remains in denial of the seriousness of the planetary crisis and the part our materialistic way of life plays in undermining the ecosystem. We rationalize away many abuses to nature and the earth because of the purported necessity of "progress" and development and our need for natural resources. Yes, we do have needs as human beings, but so do other creatures, and so does the rest of the great natural community surrounding us. Our needs must be balanced with those of other species.

Of course, far too many of our supposed needs are actually desires and wants that have been created or manipulated by the advertising industry. How many of us truly believe that we have a right to decimate the environment (with effects on humanity that almost certainly include higher disease rates and a lower quality of life) and to drive other species to extinction, simply to have more of what we don't really need in the first place?

Hope for the future clearly rests in our own hands, as well as the hands of the next couple of generations. We can't wait for others to act. According to many ecologists, a limited amount of time is left to reverse the decline of the earth's vital systems, protect endangered areas, rescue threatened species, and save our own necks—or at least reduce the possibility of massive human starvation or other catastrophic events.

Awakening to nature offers us the great gift of bringing richness and healing to our own life, but it also helps us break the hypnotic consumerist trance we've become captives of. The delusion that we can live and consume and waste without limits must be punctured. It's vital that we learn to reign in our endless wants and desires and at the same time start taking responsibility for all of life, including the many thousands of species that are on their way to becoming extinct. This doesn't mean choosing poverty, but rather simplifying our lives and limiting nonessential expenditures to those things that truly bring us satisfaction. What we have to gain from our efforts is no less than the preservation of life on this remarkable planet. Our personal problems are trivial in comparison. What, in fact, could be more important?

These are exciting and scary times to be alive. You and I and the rest of us could make a dramatic difference—in helping tip the balance in favor of protecting natural systems and curbing the exploitative elements of our society that are out of control. What exactly to do? Find appropriate actions to take. Educate yourself and others about the problems. Join environmental preservation groups, do some volunteer work to help protect or restore natural areas, and insist that your congresspeople and other leaders take firm stands for the earth. Above all, keep listening to nature's voice. Give yourself the gift of ample time to enjoy her presence, beauty, support, and nourishment. She'll let you know what needs to be done.

About the Author

Charles Cook leads hikes, wilderness trips and nature awareness retreats from March to December each year. Locations include many of the wildest and loveliest natural areas in New York, New Jersey, Connecticut, and other northeastern states. For information write to: Charles Cook, P.O. Box 655, Pomona, NY 10970; or call (845) 354-3717.